towards Land, WORK & POWER

You don't have to read any book to know that the capitalists are on the offensive, but reading books can help us figure out how to turn things around. This book is a weapon for the people, preparing all of us for the struggle to come.

— **Boots Riley**
The Coup

You hold in your hands one of the most important critical analyses of neoliberalism, U.S. empire, and the impact they are having on the urban working poor and people of color. But this compact and readable book packs much more than a brilliant critique of the current economic and political crises. Instead, *Towards Land, Work & Power* offers a strategy—a sophisticated anti-imperialist strategy that pays attention to race, gender, culture, community, immigration, and international solidarity. Veterans of many years of community and labor organizing in the San Francisco area, the folks at POWER understand "power," and what it means to fight back in the belly of the beast. This book ought to be mandatory reading for anyone committed to a politics of transformation.

— **Robin D. G. Kelley**
author of *Freedom Dreams: The Black Radical Imagination* (2002)

Towards Land, Work and Power is a gift and a challenge to people building resistance from the depths of the empire. A gift because the authors offer an incisive critique of the character and conditions of today's U.S. imperialism in a way that is both accessible and complex. A challenge because the book pushes all organizers to connect our day-to-day campaigns to the struggles for self-determination happening around the world. In the end, *Towards Land, Work, and Power* is a call to action, offering hope and vision for those of us involved in the struggles of the urban working-class and people of color.

— **Sung E Bai**
CAAAV: Organizing Asian Communities

Towards Land, Work & Power is a must read for any serious organizer attempting to formulate a strategic analysis of where and how to begin challenging international capital and the imperial state in the here and now on a local level. It is a critical and much needed bridge between the workers centers movement, the non-profit based human rights movement, and the anti-imperialist movement. *Towards Land, Work & Power* is a critical and much overdue tool needed to help fuel the resurgence of the revolutionary movement within the belly of the beast. I hope revolutionary organizers throughout the United States use it to help formulate concrete strategies to help us re-seize the initiative and advance the peoples' struggle.

— **Kali Akuno**
Malcolm X Grassroots Movement

I really didn't understand capitalism and socialism before reading this book. When I finished, I had learned a lot. I realized how the capitalist's power and wealth relies on us, the working class, assisting them in maintaining and solidifying the system. We, the working class are in the same situation all around the world where work is very difficult and hard, our incomes are the lowest, we live in places with the worst conditions. Is this the kind of life we want to live? Our basic demand to the capitalists of just and respectful compensation is not even considered. *Towards Land, Work & Power* teaches us the important lesson that our communities of color can rise up and fight for the justice and respect we deserve.

— **Fei Yi Chen**
Chinese Progressive Association

Towards Land, Work & Power is both down-to-earth and educational, realistic and optimistic, practical and inspiring. Who would think that in-depth analysis of the isms that plague our lives— capitalism, imperialism, racism, sexism, heterosexism, you name it— could be presented so clearly? The answer, I think, lies in the fact that a number of dedicated, conscious organizers have written a book to develop many more conscious organizers. Their product shines with a special energy, an irresistible passion for justice, on every page.

— **Elizabeth (Betita) Martínez**
Institute for Multi-Racial Justice

Chinese Translation: Jessy Wang, Alex T. Tom, Martin Witte
Spanish Translation: Luis Herrera, Mónica Hernestroza, Elizabeth Medrano, Marisol Ocampo
English Proofreaders: Alan Greig, Hillary Ronen, Mei-ying Ho, Caryl Browne, Pablo Soto Campoamor, Alicia Schwartz
Spanish Proofreaders: Rene Poitevin, Myriam Zamora
Chinese Proofreaders: Kathy Liu, Yi Hang Chen, Sai Jun Liang (June), Qi Wen Pan, Fei Yi Chen, Jessie Yu, King Lam Chan (King), Hong Nian Luo
Designer: Steve Williams
Chinese Layout: Jessy Wang
Printed by 1984 Printing in Oakland, CA

First Printing, March 2005
Second Printing, October 2005

LIBRARY OF CONGRESS CATALOGING-IN-PUBLLICATION DATA
Browne, Jaron; Franco, Marisa; Negrón-Gonzales, Jason; Williams, Steve
    Towards land, work & power : charting a path of resistance to u.s.-led
        imperialism / by Browne, Franco, Negrón-Gonzales, Williams—1st ed.
        p. cm.
    ISBN 0-9771911-0-9 (paperback : English)
    ISBN 0-9771911-1-7 (paperback : Spanish)
    ISBN 0-9771911-2-5 (paperback : Chinese)

Unite to Fight Press
32 Seventh Street
San Francisco, CA 94103
printing@unite-to-fight.org
www.unite-to-fight.org

Se puede comprar una versión traducida de este libro en español o chino.
本书备有中文版
This book is also available in Spanish & Chinese versions.

co-authored by
Jaron Browne, Marisa Franco, Jason Negrón-Gonzales & Steve Williams

contents

For your courageous example and the wisdom that you have given to us, *Towards Land, Work & Power* is dedicated to all of those women and men in the Third World who have and who continue to stand up for human dignity and self-determination and against U.S.-led imperialism, colonization and aggression. **We are proud to be following in your footsteps.**

We would also like to dedicate this book to all of the members of POWER. The bravery that you show to fight for a better future is an inspiration. Most special shout-outs go out to POWER's leaders and fellow travelers including Cindy, Larry, Ed, Tere, Joanne, Ace, Gloria, Don, Regina, Jordan, Donají, Garth, Bruce, Emma, Roxanne, Fuller, Nora and so many others. When the story of our people's liberation is written, you will be recognized as sheroes and heroes. **We are all proud to be in this struggle with you.**

INTRODUCTION

Here's a slum serenade, on razor blades and grenades
By nannies and maids who be polishin' the suede.
You could let the sess blow but let's make the sets grow
Into brigades with the ghetto manifesto.

— The Coup, "Ghetto Manifesto"[1]

One of an organizer's most important tasks is to help someone see the root cause of the problems that they are experiencing and to break the isolation that so many people feel. It's the task of the organizer to help someone to see that she's not the only one who went to the welfare office looking for assistance, only to get disrespectfully turned away; and to help someone to see that she's not the only one who got harassed by the police while walking her kids to the market. Ultimately, it's the organizer's job to help someone to see that changing the world is possible and that she can be a key part of making that change happen, but in the midst of major conflict, turmoil and set-backs in the United States, this ain't easy work.

We wrote *Towards Land, Work & Power* to help ourselves, and hopefully others, to make sense of what it means to be an organizer in the United States in this period of reaction and imperialist aggression. The four co-authors are all organizers with a community-labor organization called People Organized to Win Employment Rights (POWER).

Based in San Francisco, POWER is a multi-racial membership organization of low-income tenants and workers— welfare recipients, domestics, child care workers, shoe shiners, restaurant workers, unemployed folks. The members are mostly working class women and people of color who come together to fight for greater control over the conditions in their workplaces and in their communities. Since the organization was founded in 1997, we have waged and won numerous campaigns for workers rights, workplace safety, language rights, transportation justice and a raised minimum wage. To advance this work, POWER seeks to equip organizers with the practical and analytical tools they will need to carry out the organization's mission, to end poverty and oppression— once and for all.

POWER believes that the problems that we face are structural, global and historical. The system we live under produces poverty,

---

[1] The Coup, "Ghetto Manifesto," *Party Music CD*. Tommy Boy Records, 2001.

displacement and environmental destruction as mindlessly as a car engine produces exhaust, and no one organization will be able to win the changes that we need. A global social movement will be required to resolve the structural, global and historical problems of the world today.[2] While movements are always bigger than any one organization, organizations are critical pieces to the birth and growth of any movement. Just try to imagine the Civil Rights Movements without the Student Nonviolent Coordinating Committee (SNCC). Or the Anti-War Movement without the Act Now to Stop War and End Racism (ANSWER) Coalition. Organizations are the life-blood of movements, so if we want a movement then we've got to build organizations.

Organizers are the building-blocks of organization. To build strong organization, an organizer must have a broad array of skills. She must be able to connect with a diverse group of people and recruit them to get involved in the organization's work. The good organizer must also be a skilled tactician, able to help craft a winning strategy. A skilled organizer must be able to help people move through a process of leadership development where that person begins to see herself as a key part of making change happen. A lot rides on the skill of the organizer. However, the organizer needs more than just skills if she hopes to contribute to the building of a larger movement. Skills alone are not enough. An effective organizer must also have a sharp analysis of how power operates and of how change might happen within a particular system. We call those organizers who combine skill and analysis 'conscious organizers.'[3]

Conscious organizers are those organizers who self-consciously work to build organization and movement so that the people will be able to strike back at the roots causes of the problems in the

---

[2] While we do see the close relationship between organizations and movements, we do see them as two different things. We define social movements as "sustained efforts where various groups and individuals take collective and individual action to challenge authorities, power-holders or cultural beliefs for the purpose of achieving a common goal." The implication of this definition is that a movement is not made up of just one organization. By its very definition, a movement is made up of numerous organizations and individuals.

[3] We first began using the term 'conscious organizer' after a series of discussions with our comrades at the Labor Community Strategy Center.

community.[4] To fulfill her task of building organizations and a broader movement, the conscious organizer must be guided in her work by her answers to basic questions: What's the nature of the system? What are the current conditions within this system? And who are the forces that have the interest and the capability to make change?

To answer these questions, we believe that conscious organizers must develop as intellectuals. Throughout the Third World where social movements flourish, working class people, who have little formal education, study and debate theory with a prowess that would shame most college graduates in the United States. The challenges of this period demand that organizers develop the skills that are so often frowned upon. As one working class intellectual observed, "Nothing so contributes to the reproduction of class in our society, aside from property relations, as the institutionally enforced intellectual division of labor. It dissects knowledge into academic ghettos and attempts to freeze working-class people out of the intelligentsia altogether... Those of us who lack the credentials must be excluded from the intelligentsia because the inclusion of our voices [] calls into question the legitimacy of the whole system... Working-class people can and must become intellectuals. We can and must study diligently, debate, self-criticize, re-study, and continually sharpen our ability to play intellectual hardball."[5]

Sadly, there are too few conscious organizers today and there are fewer institutions which can train organizers to develop the analytic tools which would allow them to expertly play the role of a conscious organizer. If there is any realistic hope of charting a path to resist and ultimately challenge U.S.-led imperialism, that hope will depend on the ability to develop many more conscious organizers. This process of developing more conscious organizers has become an important part of our work at POWER.

---

4 When we talk about 'conscious organizers,' we are not only talking about staff organizers. Some of the best conscious organizers are not staff of any organization but are workers, young people and community members who do the work necessary to build the capacity of oppressed and exploited people to make change.

5 Stan Goff, *Full Spectrum Disorder,* 2004, page. 190.

In the summer of 2003, the organizers and leaders of POWER realized that we couldn't answer some basic questions, such as: What is the nature of the world's political economy? How do we understand the events happening around the world? How do the changes that are happening in the global political economy impact our work for racial, economic and gender justice in San Francisco? What will it take to build a broad and vibrant movement in such despondent and challenging times? In the fall of that year, the members of POWER's Amandla Project decided to answer these questions.[6] After almost twelve months of study, reflection and discussion, we had formulated answers to some of the questions that had been plaguing us. The usefulness of this study quickly became apparent as we felt better equipped to conduct our local work in a way that seemed to contribute to a global movement. By way of sharing our reflections with other conscious organizers, we decided to write down these answers.

> **We believe that change in society can only happen when two dynamics come together— when the material conditions of the world make change possible and when the capacity of the people who have an interest in making change is great enough to overcome the opposition.**

At the foundation of many of the book's ideas is our theory about how social change happens. We believe that change in society can only happen when two dynamics come together— when the material conditions of the world make change possible *and* when the capacity of the people who have an interest in making change is great enough to overcome the opposition. In other words, the window of opportunity to make change opens and closes over time. Not all moments are like every other moment. In

---

[6] In 2001, POWER created the Amandla Project (formerly named the Committee for Working Class Leadership and Strategy) to provide a space for anti-imperialist leaders and organizers to support movement building among all sectors of oppressed and exploited communities. The Amandla Project has provided a space for members to sharpen our political analysis, engage in collective action, form alliances, raise questions, and create an opening for dialogue with other no- and low-wage worker organizations and more broadly within the global movement for racial and economic justice. The members of the Committee— Marisa Franco, Jaron Browne, Jason Negrón-Gonzales and Steve Williams— are the authors of this book. Unless it's specified otherwise, when the book refers to 'we,' it is referring to the members of the Amandla Project.

order to make change, we must be able to assess when the window of opportunity is more open, **and** we must prepare ourselves to jump through the window when the opportunity presents itself.

This theory recognizes that our actions can affect these two dynamics. The people's capacity to make change is increased as organizers work to raise consciousness and build organizations and movements. Similarly, actions or campaigns which target the system's points of weakness can alter the material conditions of the world, effectively widening the window of opportunity for the people to make change.

The two dynamics are interdependent. The system will never collapse simply because the material conditions made it happen, so we don't have the luxury of just sitting back and waiting for the system's inevitable fall. The responsibility for making change lies in the hands of the people. On the other hand, change won't happen simply because the people are organized. If we act too cautiously or too aggressively because we have misread the conditions around us, our actions could serve to close the window of opportunity for change. To forward the possibly for change, the conscious organizer must be guided by the intention of acting as boldly as the conditions will allow. By building the capacity of the people and accurately assessing the material condition, we will be prepared to take bold and decisive action at opportune moments.

This theory also pushes us to clearly identify the interests of different social forces in making change. For many years, some critics within the Left have questioned why POWER has prioritized building organization amongst no- and low-wage workers. In their most generous moments, these critics are see our work with immigrant and African American workers and tenants as a noble charity. In their more skeptical moments, they question the ability of this constituency to wield the power necessary to make real change in the United States. As is evidenced by our continued work, we disagree. But we also know that we have not always been able to explain why we think that working class people of color can and will be the leading edge of an anti-imperialist movement.

We think that a sharper understanding of the world's conditions will allow us to more clearly identify which social forces have an interest in and are potentially capable of making permanent and fundamental change.

The profound changes that are happening in the world right now are forcing many of us to ask serious questions about our work, about our assessment of the world conditions, and about what it will take to win. Much of the book deals with the specific conditions that we face in San Francisco, but we believe that many of the proposals, and certainly most of the analysis, will resonate with organizers outside of the Bay Area who are grappling with these same questions of strategy and analysis.

Towards Land, Work & Power is divided into five chapters. The first chapter examines the nature of the world's political economy. It begins by looking at the capitalist system of political economy and how that system grew into today's system of political economy which we call U.S.-led imperialism. The first chapter ends by describing the challenges currently facing the system and the international ruling class. The second chapter looks at how U.S.-led imperialism plays out in the context of San Francisco and the Bay Area. Framed by the history of the City, the second chapter ends by exposing the agenda that San Francisco's ruling class is advancing in an attempt to consolidate their power and privilege. The next chapter presents the 'Towards Land, Work & Power Platform,' an alternative vision for the future of San Francisco which was developed and adopted by POWER's membership in 2003. The fourth chapter offers three strategic opportunities that we believe are critical to the growth of a strong, anti-imperialist movement inside the United States. The final chapter is a call to action, urging activists and organizers to meet the challenges and to seize the opportunities before us.

Towards Land, Work & Power is a book by conscious organizers for conscious organizers, which draws from a lot of historical documents, academic texts, political theory and policy papers. It is rooted in our shared practice as experiences building a membership organization in San Francisco's working class neighborhoods and represents our attempt to assess the racist, sexist, homophobic and inherently exploitative system of imperialism. The book uses some language that may not be familiar to a lot of organizers, but we feel that it is important for organizers to understand this language— especially the language that is used in the tradition of political organizing— because our familiarity allows us to connect with the lessons and experiences of other conscious organizers throughout history and around the globe. By getting more familiar with this language, the process of making assessments will become more accessible to all of us. Even though some of the language may be new, we believe that many of the ideas and feelings will be very familiar to anyone who is working to uproot injustice. We did not come up with many completely original ideas in the writing of this book, so you will see a lot of notes on where the ideas came from. We did this hoping that you will be encouraged you to go back, look at those materials and eventually to develop your own assessments.

To ensure that we are able to share our lessons with organizers whose preferred language is not English, we are proud that *Towards Land, Work & Power* has been translated into Spanish and written Chinese. This would not have been true if it weren't for the tireless dedication of the book's translators, Marisol Ocampo and Mónica Itzel Henestroza. Thanks also go to our allies at the Garment Workers Center, the Chinese Progressive Association and CAAAV who helped make the Spanish and Cantonese versions possible.

Like any other book, *Towards Land, Work & Power* would not have been possible without the support, both direct and indirect, of so many amazing family members and comrades. The members of the Amandla Project would like to thank all of those who have taught us and helped us become the organizers that we are today. Specifically, we would like to acknowledge our compañeras and compañeros at the Miami Workers Center, the Labor Community Strategy Center, Direct Action for Rights and Equality, the Tenants and Workers Support Committee, and CAAAV: Organizing Asian Communities. It is because of the example of your inspiring practice and principled struggle that we were able to sharpen our ideas in the way that we have. As first-time authors whose propensity for spelling and typographical errors seemed to have no limit, we would like to extend our heart-felt appreciation to our dedicated team of proof-readers which included Hillary Ronen, Mei-ying Ho, Caryl Browne, Pablo Soto Campoamor, Alicia Schwartz and Alan Greig.

We recognize that because of limited time and resources, this book is limited. But we believe that we have been able to consolidate and combine existing information, and innovate some new ideas that have important ramifications for all of our work. In the end, we hope that *Towards Land, Work & Power* will spark productive conversation and debate that can advance our collective capacity to produce winning strategy, conscious organizers and strong fighting organizations. We also hope that people can give us feedback to help us further clarify our analysis.

After our long study, we are very hopeful about the possibility for change, and we don't think that we're alone in thinking that the possibility for radical change is growing. Even *Business Week* can see it when they remind us, "Every once in a great while, the established order is overthrown. Within a span of decades, technological advances, organizational innovations, and new ways of thinking transform economies... On the eve of the twenty-first century, the signs of monumental change are all around us."[7]

Without any further ado, we humbly offer the conclusions of our investigation to the movement, and in particular to those organizers and activists across the San Francisco Bay Area who have made the Bay Area such a good place to do this work. May this book help to prepare movement to move all of our communities towards land, work and power.

---

[7] *Business Week,* January 1995.

chapter one
it's the economy

That dark and vast sea of human labor in China and India, the South Seas and all Africa; in the West Indies and Central America and in the United States— that great majority of [humanity] on whose bent and broken backs rest today the founding stones of modern industry— shares a common destiny; it is despised and rejected by race and color; paid a wage below the level of the decent living; driven, beaten, prisoned and enslaved in all but name; spawning the world's raw material and luxury— cotton, wool, coffee, tea, cocoa, palm oil, fibers, spices, rubber, silks, lumber, copper, gold, diamonds, leather— how shall we end the list and where? All these are gathered up at prices lowest of the low, manufactured, transformed and transported at fabulous gain; and the resultant wealth is distributed and displayed and made the basis of world power and universal dominion and armed arrogance in London and Paris, Berlin and Rome, New York and Rio de Janeiro.

Here is the real modern labor problem. Here is the kernel of the problem of Religion and Democracy, of Humanity. Words and futile gestures avail nothing. Out of the exploitation of the dark proletariat comes the Surplus Value filched from human beasts which, in cultured lands, the Machine and harnessed Power veil and conceal. The emancipation of [humanity] is the emancipation of labor and the emancipation of labor is the freeing of that basic majority of workers who are yellow, brown and black.

— W.E.B. DuBois[1]

Dr. W.E.B. Dubois' words, written in 1935, paint a powerful picture of the world that still resonate today. Seven decades later, in our world of "globalization," a failed "new economy" and a supposed "war or terror," Dr. Dubois' words still cut to the core of our world situation where extreme wealth is made possible because of the exploitation of "that dark and vast sea of human labor" in the Global South. We still live in a world where the people of the Global South create the products and wealth enjoyed by the rich nations, and we still live in a world where Middle Eastern, African, Latin American and Asian people, wherever they live in the world confront the "armed arrogance" of the world's imperialist super-power.

The ruling elite of the rich nations claim that the system of capitalism is a system of freedom and prosperity. The advances the world has seen under capitalism are undeniable. Medicine. Communications. Transportation. Science. Capitalism has developed the productive capacity so that all of humanity's basic needs could be met. You would expect that such advancements would lift living standards for everyone so that no one should want for basic food, shelter, medical care and education. Instead, we are witness to unprecedented levels of poverty, unemployment, displacement, disease and environmental degradation in a period where the world has witnessed unprecedented advances.

The ruling elite claim that the global economy creates prosperity and jobs. But we see a world where three billion people, or half of the world's population, live on under two dollars a day; 1.3 billion have no access to clean water; three billion have no access to sanitation; two billion have no access to electricity.[2] We see more than 11 million children dying each year from preventable causes.[3]

---

[1] W.E.B. DuBois, *Black Reconstruction in America, 1860 – 1880.* 1935.

[2] James Wolfenson, *The Other Crisis,* World Bank, October 1998, quoted from *The Reality of Aid 2000,* (Earthscan Publications, 2000), p.10.

[3] These statistics on global poverty, inequity, and death from preventable diseases are widely published and available. Even Kofi Annan, Secretary-General of the United Nations, said in a 2003 address, "I feel angry, I feel distressed, I feel helpless— to live in a world where we have the means, we have the resources, to be able to help []— what is lacking is the political will."

They claim that the United States is the land of opportunity. This is a lie too. We see more than 44 million people who lack health coverage and over 3 million women, children and men who are homeless.[4] We see unemployment rates soaring above 60% in many African American communities. We see more and more people crammed into welfare offices, decrepit schools and state-of-the-art prisons. We see our family members pulled into an economic draft to drop bombs on poor nations all over the Global South.

Politicians pat themselves on the back for all of the progress that they are making. Meanwhile, we see the gulf between rich and poor widening everyday. Just twenty percent of the world's population in the First World nations consume 86% of the world's goods.[5] How do we make sense of this gross inequality?

Many times in our organizing work, we hear working class people talk about those in power like they are just well meaning incompetents. They'll say, "If only the people in power understood what poor people go through, then they'd make things better." We think that gives them credit that they don't deserve. Those in power are well aware of the depths of misery and oppression that the majority of humanity experience everyday. They simply choose not to do anything about it because they have pledged their allegiance to defending the interests of a system that makes a small number of people rich and powerful—at the direct expense of the planet and the people of the world. Just like a freezer can't bake a cake, capitalism doesn't produce equality.

It doesn't have to be this way. The world's economy produces enough food to end hunger. There is more than enough vacant housing to provide shelter for all homeless people. Each year the people of the United States spend three times more money on cosmetics, jewelry and pet food than what it would cost to provide education, clean water and medical care to everyone around the world who needs it.[6] Humanity has the potential to successfully

---

[4] National Coalition for the Homeless Fact Sheet.

[5] *1998 Human Development Report,* United Nations Development Programme.

[6] Osvaldo Martinez, "Speech at the 2003 World Social Forum," Porto Alegre, Brazil; January 27, 2003.

combat the diseases that kill millions of people each year. The problem is not that we lack the capacity to meet the needs of the people. The problem is that poverty, inequality and repression are known and accepted effects of the profit driven system that we live under. As we said in the introduction, if we want to make change then we must build the capacity of the people to make change and we have to understand the conditions in which we find ourselves to know what change is strategic at this moment.

The political economy of a given society makes up the material conditions of that society.[7] Political economy is the way a society produces, distributes and consumes goods and services as well as the structures and ideologies which that society uses to maintain and reinforce this system. The political economy of today's world is a unique and advanced form of capitalism referred to as imperialism. In order to understand imperialism, we have to first understand the political economy of capitalism.

adventures in capitalism

Emerging out of the feudal system in Western Europe and European colonization of Africa, Asia and the Americas in the early part of the 15th century, the capitalist system is the foundation of contemporary imperialism.[8] Capitalism is a system of political economy characterized by socialized production of commodities and private appropriation of profit. In other words, capitalist production is set up so that everyone plays a particular role in the production of the society's goods and services. This is what is meant by 'socialized production.' On the other hand, 'private appropriation' means that only a small group of individuals takes the value produced by society's labor.

---

[7] In saying this, we mean that the development of the political economy of a society has a foundational role in shaping where people are and what they do. The culture, ideas and customs of a given society are shaped by the structure of that society's political economy.

[8] In the mid-1800s a German intellectual named Karl Marx set about theorizing capitalism, which he was witnessing expand all around him. His masterpiece, *Capital*, lays out an insightful assessment of the capitalist political economy that we feel is fundamental to understanding the system. This section draws heavily from his ideas.

> **From the theft of gold and land from the peoples of the Americas to the enslavement of African people to the invisibilizing of women's work in the home, capitalism's acquisition of its means of production— land, labor and resources— has always been based on the exploitation and subjugation of people of color and women.**

In order to do this socialized production, the capitalist political economy feeds on the fuel of three basic ingredients: land, labor and resources. These three ingredients are called the 'means of production.' Without any of the means of production, a society cannot produce goods and services. This is why the capitalist system has historically been, and continues to be, ruthless in its quest to steal, acquire and commandeer the land, labor and resources that it needs. From the theft of gold and land from the peoples of the Americas, to the enslavement of African people, to the invisibilizing of women's work in the home, capitalism's acquisition of its means of production— land, labor and resources— has always been based on the exploitation and subjugation of people of color and women.

Under capitalism, a small group of individuals controls the means of production of that entire society. The result is a class-based society in which some people work in order to live while others live off of the labor of those working people. According to Marx's analysis, one's class position is determined by how that person fits into the process of capitalist production— not necessarily by how much money someone makes, or even if that person is currently employed.[9] Those who own the means of production

---

[9] Here, we think that it is helpful to hear directly from Marx as he described the formation of classes. This excerpt is taken from his essay "Wage Labour and Capital" which he wrote in 1847:

> "In the process of production, human beings work not only upon nature, but also upon one another. They produce only by working together in a specified manner and reciprocally exchanging their activities. In order to produce, they enter into definite connections and relations to one another, and only within these social connections and relations does their influence upon nature operate — i.e., does production take place.

> "These social relations between the producers, and the conditions under which they exchange their activities and share in the total act of production, will naturally vary according to the character of the means of production."

are the capitalist class.[10] Those who don't own the means of production make up the working class.[11] Because they do not own the tools and materials to meet their own needs, each member of the working class is forced to sell her or his 'labor power' in exchange for wages.[12] Capitalism doesn't give working class people any other choice- work for wages or starve.

As capitalism began to develop in Europe in the 15th century, budding capitalists had to struggle to find workers who wanted to come work in their factories because on the feudal estates people had the means to subsist by working the land. To get people to come off the land, the capitalists employed brute force to seize land that had previously been held and worked on by peasant farmers. Without the means to subsist on their own, peasants were literally forced to sell their labor to the capitalists. Around the globe whenever and wherever capitalism emerged, peasants have resisted this process. But with brutal and bloody force, the capitalists were able to construct a working class by forcing peasants off the land, into the city and into their factories.[13] As Marx concludes, "Thus were the agricultural people, first forcibly

---

[10] In his analysis of the capitalist system, Karl Marx refers to the working class as the 'proletariat' and to the capitalist class as the 'bourgeoisie'. We here are using the phrase "capitalist class" to highlight this aspect of being the class that lives by its ownership of capital and the means of production.

[11] Marx writes that the two most important classes in a capitalist society are the capitalist and working classes. However, he also acknowledges that there are finer gradations in capitalist class structure. For example, Marx identifies doctors who have their own practices as members of the petit bourgeoisie class. The translation from the French means little bourgeoisie, and that's how Marx talked about them. They were able to work for themselves because of the skills that they had acquired, but did not hire employees on the scale of the bourgeoisie. In his writings, Marx points out dozens of classes, from the land-owning class to the lumpen proletariat all of whom he says relate to society's process of production, distribution and consumption differently.

[12] 'Labor power' is the term that Marx uses to describe a workers' ability to work. This is what the worker actually sells to the capitalist; the ability to work. It is then the capitalists responsibility to get the worker to use her labor power to produce commodities that the capitalist can sell. This is different from piece work where employees are paid for each commodity that she produces. In traditional structures of capitalist employment, the capitalist is paying for the worker's ability to work over a particular time so if eventually the capitalist purchases technology which allows the worker to produce more commodities in the same amount of time, there is no need for the capitalist to give a raise to the worker.

[13] In Marx, this process is known as "primitive accumulation." Other writers such as David Harvey have pointed out that this process is an ongoing part of capitalist growth and doesn't just fade away after the transition from feudalism is complete. Harvey has called this process "accumulation through dispossession," and has referred to the United States' war on Iraq as a classic example of this process of accumulation by way of brute force.

expropriated from the soil, driven from their homes, turned into vagabonds, and then whipped, branded, tortured by laws grotesquely terrible, into the discipline necessary for the wage system."[14]

The fact that you have lost your ability to produce food to feed your family doesn't mean that capitalism guarantees that there will be a job for you. On the contrary, capitalism is not capable of providing jobs for every member of the working class. And that's intentional. The system creates a pool of unemployed and under-employed workers. Marx called this pool the 'reserve army of labor.' The reserve army of labor is necessary to allow the capitalists to drive down wages and worsen conditions for those members of the working class who do have jobs. If workers demand higher wages or better working conditions, capitalists can threaten to replace them with an unemployed worker. It is this threat that often keeps workers going back to work for the capitalist, based on the reality that in capitalism a small paycheck is better than no paycheck.

The capitalist class employs workers and employs the means of production to make commodities. Marx was the first to observe that commodities are the building blocks of capitalism; the life-blood of the capitalist system. A commodity is any good or service that is produced for the purpose of being sold or exchanged for something else. Everything is a commodity in a capitalist system. From a loaf of bread, to a one-bedroom house, to the labor used to clean that house, everything is treated like a commodity under capitalism.

Once in the factories, sweatshops or whatever the workplace is called, the worker receives a wage to produce commodities that are then considered to be the property of the capitalist. The boss tries to sell them for a price that is greater than the total of the wages plus the cost of the materials that the worker used to produce the commodity; keeping for himself the surplus above the wage he paid the worker. This surplus value comes to the capitalist class because the owner pays the worker less than the value of what she produces.

---

[14] Karl Marx. *Capital,* Vol. I, Part VIII.

To illustrate this point, let's look at the example of Maria, one member of the working class, who is hired to make chairs by Mr. Blanco, a member of the capitalist class.[15] Mr. Blanco pays Maria $8 per hour for an eight-hour day. At the end of the day, Maria will receive $64 in wages. In that time, Maria will finish building sixteen chairs, two each hour. If each chair sells for $15, Mr. Blanco will bring in $240. If the materials for the chairs cost $2 per chair, then Mr. Blanco will clear a profit of $144 in one day by simply paying Maria less in wages than the market value of the commodities that she produced.

Mr. Blanco's Daily Exploitation of Maria

Hour	1	2	3	4	5	6	7	8	TOTAL
Wages	8	8	8	8	8	8	8	8	$64
Prod. Cost	2+2	2+2	2+2	2+2	2+2	2+2	2+2	2+2	$32
Sale Price	15+15	15+15	15+15	15+15	15+15	15+15	15+15	15+15	$240
Net Profit	18	18	18	18	18	18	18	18	$144

This is called wage exploitation and, in capitalism, wage exploitation is the fundamental way that profits are made. This wage exploitation happens for every worker that the capitalists hire. Thus, in every store and every factory of capitalist society, bosses get rich by underpaying the workers. In our example, Mr. Blanco appropriates $144 every day from each worker he employs. Mr. Blanco, the capitalist class and the capitalist system could not survive without the wage exploitation of the working class. This is why we say that capitalism is an inherently exploitative system.

Once the capitalist takes what the worker produced, he sells it to whoever is willing and able to buy it. When the commodity is sold, the profits stay with the capitalist even though it was the worker's labor that produced it. The logic of the system is that since the capitalist bought the materials and the labor of the worker, then the capitalist should keep the profits and the worker should be grateful.

It is this pursuit of profit that drives production in the capitalist system. Things are not made just to be used. To be sold, commodities must be useful to someone, yet that is not the

---

[15] This illustration was originally developed by the School of Unity and Liberation (SOUL).

central concern of the capitalists. They do not hire the working class to produce commodities so that those commodities can meet some unmet need within society. Food is not grown to feed people. Housing is not built to shelter people. Medicine is not produced to make people healthy. Under capitalism, everything is produced for profit. As a result, capitalism's colossal means of production are driven to produce luxury items that society doesn't need. The examples are all around us. While millions of African and Asian people die of a treatable virus, U.S.-based pharmaceutical companies spend billions trying to perfect the formula for Viagra.

According to the logic of the capitalist system, it is better to destroy a commodity if it cannot be sold for a profit so that workers are unable to meet their needs without depending on selling their labor. There are lots of examples of this happening. One of the best known took place in the United States during the Great Depression of the 1930s when huge stockpiles of food were burned as millions of people went hungry.

Because profit and not need drives the system, there is no planning what a society produces. The capitalist class produces stuff because they think that they'll be able to sell it, whatever it is: town houses, chocolate ice cream or Hello Kitty stickers. Marx called this system of production the 'anarchy of the market.'

CAPITALISM'S CORE NEEDS

Under capitalism, the capitalist class is in a never-ending rat race trying to track down the biggest profit. They are constantly seeking bigger sources of profit because the capitalists are competing with each other.

To grow faster and out-perform their competitors, each member of the capitalist class is constantly looking for newer and better ways to exploit the working class. Most often, the capitalists look to increase their profit by reducing the cost of production. The capitalists reduce their cost of production by three ways: by cutting workers' wages, by re-organizing their factory to make it more efficient, or by bringing in new tools or machinery that allow the workers to produce more commodities in less time thereby driving down the cost of production.

The most efficient of these three options for the capitalist is to extract more profits from the working class by 'revolutionizing the means of production.' Using our previous example again, if Mr. Blanco buys a machine that allows Maria to produce twice as many chairs over the course of a day, then he will dramatically increase his profits (assuming he can sell the chairs) because Maria's wages and the cost of the materials for each chair are both remaining constant. This points to the first of capitalism's three core needs: the need to constantly revolutionize the means of production. Capitalism needs to develop more and more efficient tools so that the capitalist class can extract the profits that they need to survive.

While revolutionizing the means of production is an effective way to extract profit, it is also problematic for Mr. Blanco because the cost of buying a new machine will cut into whatever profits he has accumulated. Sooner or later, Mr. Blanco will not have a choice. He will either improve his means of production or face going out of business because of the competition inherent in the capitalist system. Whether or not Mr. Blanco purchases the new machine, some other capitalist will, and in doing so will be able to sell the chairs for less than $10 and still make the same profit. If this happens, most people will buy the chairs that cost less, and Mr. Blanco will be left with a bunch of chairs that he can't sell. If this goes on too long, Mr. Blanco will either go out of business or else his competitor will buy out Mr. Blanco's company. This leads us to the second of capitalism's core needs: the need for ever-expanding profits. Every capitalist needs to bring in more and more profits so that they will be able to improve the means of production so that he can drive down the cost of production. This is necessary because the capitalists face constant competition from other members of the capitalist class. Every capitalist has to grow or else face the possibility of their own extinction.

By revolutionizing the means of production, larger capitalists make it possible for the workers to produce more and more chairs. But eventually they run out of people who can buy all of these chairs that are produced. After all, being able to produce twice as many chairs doesn't mean that there are twice as many people who will buy them. The capitalist has still got to sell in order to make a profit. This leads to the third core need of capitalism: the need to expand to new markets. Because Mr. Blanco still has to sell chairs to realize a profit, he looks to expand to new markets in a different city or in a different country.

CAPITALIST PATRIARCHY

As capitalism developed and workers were driven into wage labor for their survival, not all work was equally valued or even deemed worthy of wages. Capitalism emerged out of a violently patriarchal system that had existed in Europe for hundreds of years. Under feudalism land was held by a specific class of men. A man from this class was thought to own not only his plot of land, but also all of the servants who worked his land, as well as his wife and family.[16] Women were considered the property of their fathers until they married and then became the property of their husbands.

This class division of human society between men and women provided the groundwork for capitalist exploitation of women as wage-workers who could be paid less for their work in the workplace, and nothing at all for their work in the home. As we discussed earlier in this chapter, the capitalist political economy relies on workers who can be exploited as they produce commodities. But in order to work and produce surplus value, workers must also eat, sleep and be healthy. They must feed, clothe and educate their children. Capitalism doesn't only need workers to produce on a daily basis, but the system also needs workers to reproduce for the future. This process is called the reproduction of the working class— that is, the work of birthing, feeding, cleaning, clothing, sheltering, nurturing, educating, nursing, etc. Through patriarchy, reproductive labor isn't even understood as work. Instead, it's cast as the "free" and "natural" activities that women are supposed to do as wives, mothers and daughters because it is an extension of their inherent way of being.

---

[16] Frederick Engels, "The Origin of the Family, Private Property and the State," 1884.

This gendered division of labor is critical for the capitalists because they cannot sustain the system without the reproduction of the working class, but at the same time they can't afford to pay for all of this work. In order to satisfy their needs, capitalism transformed the family.[17] The family became, and in many ways continues to be, the social tool through which the gendered reproduction of the working class would be carried out— to directly benefit the capitalist class, without demanding any compensation from the capitalist class.

The nuclear family was defined, socially and legally, as the union of a man and a woman. Each partner had their particular role to fill according to the gendered norms of this patriarchal system. The working class man was to sell his labor to the capitalist class so that he could bring home a wage to provide for himself, his wife and their future workers, also known as children. The working class woman was to do the work necessary for the reproduction of her working class family. Even the work that women do outside of the home is impacted by their position as secondary class citizens. While working class families have long required the income of multiple workers to generate enough wages to support a family, women's work is generally considered supplemental income for male family breadwinners. Entire industries that are considered women's work, such as the textile industry, service and clerical work, are paid less. Under capitalist patriarchy, these sectors have been "housewifized" and occupy the lowest-waged sectors of work.[18]

This system, which is so deeply invested in the definition of a nuclear family as a relationship of a man and a woman, was and is extremely threatened by any behavior that falls outside of this definition in any way. As a result, capitalism is a patriarchal system that oppresses gay, lesbian, bisexual and trans-gendered people as it does women. The result of the system's need to mask and exploit women's labor is that capitalism attempts to force

---

[17] Frederick Engels, "The Origin of the Family, Private Property and the State," 1884.

[18] Maria Mies, in *Patriarchy and Accumulation on a World Scale,* explained housewifization as this process of class formation under capitalist patriarchy and the invisibilizing of women's labor. This model of super-exploitation, intertwined with the rise of white supremacy, was foundational to colonialism and the theft of Third World labor.

everyone— by way of socialization, coercion and violence— into a narrow and artificial gender binary.

The unpaid labor of women— enforced through compulsory heterosexuality and a rigid gender binary— benefits men by elevating their class position within society and the family, and benefits the system of capitalism as a whole by ensuring that the reproduction of the working class continues without any expense to the capitalist class. In this way, capitalism was built directly on the foundation of patriarchy and has only ever been patriarchal, and the process of making women's work invisible has been and continues to be an inseparable part of the class structure of capitalism.

CRISIS FOR CAPITALISM, OPPORTUNITY FOR WORKING CLASS

The capitalist system periodically suffers from slow growth, rising costs, high unemployment, stagnant job creation and instability for businesses. The defenders of the system argue that these are simply aberrations of an otherwise divine system. But they are wrong. Crisis is actually built into the genetic fiber of capitalism. Capitalist crisis occurs when, for whatever reason, the system fails to extract the level of profits that it needs. The irony is that as capitalism increases its capacity to produce more and more commodities, the system becomes less and less stable. In many ways, the system's own success brings about crisis.

The capitalist system is vulnerable to two, inter-related forms of crisis: the crisis of over-production and the crisis of the tendency for the rate of profit to fall. The crisis of over-production describes the situation when too many goods have been produced for the system to consume. This happens because the capitalist system is constantly advancing its ability to produce commodities without advancing the ability of consumers to buy those commodities. This creates a crisis for the capitalists because they are not able to realize profit if they are not able to sell their commodities. As a result, goods lie on the shelves, "production grinds to a halt, people lose their jobs," and demand drops even more.[19]

---

[19] Encyclopedia of Marxism Website, (http://www.marxists.org/glossary/terms/o/v.htm.)

The crisis of the tendency for the rate of profit to fall is the dynamic that Marx observed that "the rate of profit enjoyed by capitalists will get smaller and smaller over time."[20] He suggested that this would happen because as capitalists employ more and more advanced technologies in the production process, they will use less and less human labor-power. Because profits fundamentally come from the exploitation of human labor in capitalism, the capitalist's rate of profit would fall over time.[21] It's like capitalism has a built-in Catch-22. If the capitalists don't use the latest and greatest technologies, they will likely be taken over by some other capitalist but on the other hand, if they do jump on the technology bandwagon they are cutting down on the rate of profit that they will be able to extract.

> In a rational world, the introduction of technology would be a good thing. Things would be produced for the purpose of meeting people's needs, and it would take less time to do it. But capitalism does not produce a rational world and meeting people's needs is not the capitalists' motivation.

In a rational world, the introduction of technology would be a good thing. Things would be produced for the purpose of meeting people's needs, and it would take less time to do it. But capitalism does not produce a rational world and meeting people's needs is not the capitalists' motivation. In this form of political economy, commodities are produced in order to reap a profit. As a result of this dynamic, the system is constantly veering towards crisis.[22] The capitalist class is constantly pushing and pulling on different parts of the political economy— like interest rates, worker protections, government spending, etc.— in a desperate attempt to steer the system away the ever-looming crises. Nevertheless, because crisis is an inherent part of the system, the system regularly falls into some form of crisis despite the best efforts of the capitalist class.

---

[20] Encyclopedia of Marxism Website, (http://www.marxists.org/glossary/frame.htm.).

[21] Encyclopedia of Marxism Website, (http://www.marxists.org/glossary/terms/o/v.htm.).

[22] Between 1834 and 1991, the political economy of the United States underwent thirty-five crises as a part of the regular business cycles. Only two of those crises— from 1873 – 1893 and 1929 – 41— were severe enough to be considered depressions. (Tom Bottomore, editor, *A Dictionary of Marxist Thought* (Second Edition), p. 160).

Not surprisingly, different classes are affected by capitalism's crises differently. During these periods, it is the working class that bears the brunt of the system's dysfunction. Working people lose jobs and see inflation eat away the purchasing power of their wages. Nevertheless, the crisis is in reality a crisis of the system. Usually, capitalist crises are relatively small and do not throw the entire system into turmoil. However, when the capitalists are unsuccessful in finding a way to avoid a severe crisis, which can be because of lots of different reasons, including capitalist mismanagement or because of heightened class struggle, the capitalist system becomes fragile and more vulnerable to the demands of the working class for reform or radical social transformation. It is for this reason that, even though the impacts of crisis fall on the backs of the working class and oppressed nationalities, we say that crisis for the capitalist system really represents opportunity for anti-imperialist forces.

In summary, capitalism is an inherently exploitative and patriarchal system of production, distribution and consumption. In this system one class of people grows wealthy off of the wealth created by another class of people. The capitalist system of political economy has three core needs:

1) *the need to constantly revolutionize the means of production;*
2) *the need for ever-expanding profits; and*
3) *the need to expand to new markets.*

If capitalism is able to meet these needs, it grows. Accumulating more and more profit, the process of growth piles greater and greater sums of money into the hands of the capitalist class, who in turn gobble up their competitors as fast as possible. Small businesses become monopolies that then become transnational corporations. The success of the system means that capitalism itself must be transformed. In order to survive, it eventually transformed into something even more exploitative and global, something called imperialism.

imperialism is capitalism all grown up

The political economy of the world today is best described as imperialism. Imperialism is, at its core, an advanced stage of capitalism which thrives off of exploitation in the same way that capitalism does. What changes from capitalism to imperialism is the shape and scale of the system. For example, where the basic unit of exploitation is between the worker and the capitalist under capitalism, under imperialism the basic unit of exploitation shifts to nations exploiting whole peoples.

Imperialism takes many forms— cultural, economic, military, political, etc.— which are different but inter-related. All of these forms act in concert with one another, effectively allowing a small group of nations to control the resources, land, labor and markets of the rest of the world. Imperialism has re-shaped the language, culture and future of the majority of the people of the world; and it continues to impact our development to this very day.[23]

In the course of our study, we developed this definition of imperialism:

> *Imperialism is a global system of political economy based on the super-exploitation of whole nations and peoples by the world's imperial powers and transnational corporations. To sustain this unstable multi-national system, the imperialist state serves as a manager for global capital.*

We're now going to break this definition down so that we understand its implications:

> *Imperialism is a global system of political economy...*

Like all other systems of political economy, imperialism shapes how a society produces, distributes and consumes its goods

---

[23] We developed these ideas after a series of conversations with staff and members from CAAAV: Organizing Asian Communities in New York City.

and services. The globalized imperialist political economy is just an advanced stage of capitalism. Like its predecessor, the imperialist system divides humanity on the basis of those who produce wealth and those who exploit the producers of wealth. Imperialism depends on the constant revolutionizing of the means of production. Imperialism is driven by the need for ever-expanding profit and markets. Today's imperialism is not just a set of policies; it is not just how the United States bullies the rest of the world. Imperialism is a system driven by the insatiable quest for more and more profits.

Imperialism, as a system, really took hold when capitalism began to outgrow its national operations and became more and more of a global system. Until the end of the 19th century, capitalism was largely a national system of exploitation of the working class by the capitalist class. But capitalism had to break out of its national borders like a snake that had outgrown its skin. With the development of new technologies such as the steam engine and electricity, the capitalist class was able to produce more commodities than they could sell in just their national markets. The system had to grow or die.

This period, from 1846 to 1898, saw major technological breakthroughs and unprecedented imperialist expansion. The assembly line allowed one worker to complete nine cars in the time that it once took to build one. National railroad systems were set up, connecting disparate parts of the United States. All of these advances in society's productive capacity resulted in the capitalists having more commodities that they needed to get off their hands. The resulting economic warfare of competition went hand-in-hand with political warfare and conquest of nations. The capitalist class attempted to deal with these crises by seizing numerous foreign territories.[24] During this time period, Europe expanded its colonial control of Africa from 10% in 1870 to 90% in 1890.[25] The United States annexed half of Mexico's territory in 1848, and then went to war with Spain in 1898 to snatch up

---

[24] The crises of the imperialist political economy are very closely related to the crises of the capitalist system. We will examine imperialism's crises later on in this chapter.

[25] Answers.com Website, (http://www.answers.com/topic/scramble-for-africa).

colonies in Puerto Rico, Guam and the Philippines. The expansion of the European and U.S. empires gave the growing imperialist powers direct control over additional markets and sources of raw materials.

> *... based on the super-exploitation of whole nations and peoples by the world's imperial powers and transnational corporations.*

As we reviewed earlier, capitalism is driven by the capitalist class' exploitation of the working class. Imperialism too is driven by exploitation, but imperialist exploitation takes place on a different scale and in different forms.

Imperialist exploitation takes place on a world-scale, and transnational corporations are one of the primary vehicles for carrying out that exploitation. As we mentioned earlier, larger capitalists buy out smaller capitalists. In the transition from capitalism to imperialism, larger capitalist corporations achieve monopolistic control over certain markets. With their expansion to additional markets across the globe, transnational corporations are newly able to move their production to different countries— to get the lowest wages or to avoid environmental protections— always with the goal of extracting more profit. In today's world, some corporations have larger profits than entire countries. For example, General Motors, Exxon and Wal-Mart are each larger than the economies of Denmark, South Africa, or Indonesia.[26] In fact, of the world's one-hundred largest economic entities, fifty-one are corporations. Corporations play a critical role under global imperialism. Nevertheless, despite their immense power and influence, monopolies and transnational corporations still rely heavily on the imperialist state.

This system is maintained by the imperialist nations' exploitation of other nations and whole peoples. With the globalization of the world's production and consumption, imperialist nations rely on other nations as necessary sites to facilitate the production and realization of profit. At different stages in history, these

---

[26] Corporate Accountability Project Website, (http://www.corporations.org/system/top100.html).

under-developed nations were regarded as sources of cheap (or free for the taking) resources and labor, dumping grounds for excess commodities or as cash cows. This is not to say that the exploitation of the working class ends. The working class of all nations continue to be exploited under imperialism. But under imperialism, that exploitation takes place within the context of the super-exploitation of under-developed nations. The super-exploitation of nations becomes the driving force of the world's political economy.[27]

Super-exploitation has taken many different forms throughout history. Initially, the imperialist nations just stole from other nations. This was the case with Spanish conquistadors' theft of gold and other precious metals from the Americas. This was the case with the British theft of Native American land. It was the case with British, Spanish, Portuguese and Dutch theft of Africans to be used as slave labor throughout the Americas. Later, imperial powers seized control of colonies to use as forced consumers of the imperial powers' excess production, a guaranteed mechanism to stave off the crisis of over-production. Today, the under-developed nations are used as sources of wealth for the imperial nations, sometimes as producers and almost always as cash cows, sending billions of dollars to rich countries as debt re-payment.

Super-exploitation is possible because of the deliberate under-development of the non-imperialist nations. Through theft, warfare, sanctions and forced debt, imperialist nations deliberately under-develop other nations so that those nations will be compelled to create surplus wealth for the imperialist nations, just as the working class creates surplus for the capitalist class under capitalism. As writers including Walter Rodney, Eduardo Galeano, Vandana Shiva and Samir Amin have all documented, the world's imperialist powers have a long and bloody record of undermining and sabotaging the development of strong economies and viable systems in oppressed nations all around the

---

[27] We refer to the extraction of surplus value in the imperialist system as "super-exploitation" because the rate of exploitation is much greater and the methods are more varied when compared to capitalist exploitation. Because the imperialist class does not feel as responsible for the reproduction of under-developed nations, the rate of exploitation in the Global South far exceeds that which normally takes place within capitalism. It also takes more forms than just wage exploitation as we describe.

globe.[28] By enslaving the people of the Global South, waging war and imposing structural adjustment through the International Monetary Fund and the World Bank, the imperialist nations ensure that no viable economy can ever develop. They then turn around and claim that their domination is necessary because the "under-developed" nations aren't capable of governing themselves! They have condemned the majority of the world to a life-sentence of crippling poverty and benefit from this by extracting super-profits from workers of the under-developed nations to support the decadent lifestyles of people within the empires. Imperialist nations do this because they want servants, not competitors.

By handing out small crumbs for privileged sections of society and holding out the ever-present threat of violence, the imperialist nations use an elaborate array of carrots and sticks to organize the consent of whoever they can for the purpose of maintaining this relationship. The imperial powers go to such great lengths because the under-development of the oppressed nations is necessary for the over-development and wealth of the imperialist nations. This is one of the central features of the imperialist political economy: it develops nations unevenly. Not all nations can be wealthy. Imperialist nations enjoy tremendous wealth and prosperity only because they suck off the wealth and resources of the under-developed nations like a parasite. Under imperialism, the large majority of nations are made poor so that they are forced to serve the interests of the imperialist nations.

The imperialist world system itself did not develop in a vacuum. Growing out of colonial pillage and patriarchal repression, imperialism continues to have its own enabling forms of oppression. White supremacy and the European conquest provided today's

---

[28] All of these writers have examined the imperialist system's impact on the people outside of the empire. Walter Rodney (1942 – 1980) was a Guyanese historian and political activist who wrote the important book *How Europe Underdeveloped Africa*. Eduardo Galeano (1940 - Present) is a Uruguayan writer who exposed the centuries of pillage in his work, *Open Veins of Latin America*. Dr. Vandana Shiva (1952 - Present) is an Indian physicist, ecologist, activist, editor and author of many books including *Stolen Harvest: The Hijacking of the Global Food Supply* and *Staying Alive : Women, Ecology and Development*. Samir Amin (1931 – Present) is an Egyptian-born political economist who has a reputation as one of the most insightful writers about the issues arising out of the changing nature of capitalism. His work includes *Accumulation on a World Scale* and *The Liberal Virus: Permanent War and the Americanization of the World*.

imperialist nations with the foundation of their wealth and power. European and white settler nations who set about conquering and enslaving found in white supremacy the ideological justification for the pillaging, enslavement and genocide of the peoples of Africa, Asia and the Americas.

The historical development of imperialism alongside the history of European conquest has produced today's imperialist system which is always racist. The reality of imperialism is fundamentally racist, and imperialist super-exploitation is justified and rationalized through racism. Imperialism's inhumane brutality is heaped upon people who are portrayed as less than human.[29] The very way in which the system extracts wealth is racist. Look at the example of free trade zones in Jamaica, Zimbabwe, Mexico or Panama where thousands of women work in factories at below poverty wages. As patriarchy does with capitalism, white supremacy has been and continues to be a fundamental part of the imperialist system. So when thinking about ending the imperialist political economy, one must also fight the racist, sexist, homophobic and transphobic aspects of the system.

Although the super-exploitation of nations fuels the imperialist system, this doesn't mean that imperialism is only international. The imperialist system, and the super-exploitation of whole peoples, plays out within imperialist nations too. Let's take the example of the United States.

The self-perpetuated myth is that the United States is a welcome home for people from every corner of the globe. However, the reality is that the United States is not one, unified nation.[30] The people who live in this country do not live in similar conditions, and we do not share the same interests. Within the borders of this

---

[29] This idea is drawn from the ideas developed by Franz Fanon; see *The Wretched of the Earth*.

[30] Even sectors of the ruling class recognize that there are different nations within the borders of this country. Most recently, Senator John Edwards made the reality of 'two Americas" the central platform of his 2004 presidential campaign. However, John Edwards was far from the first member of the ruling class to talk about two Americas. In 1896, the Supreme Court ruled that maintaining two separate nations was acceptable as long as those nations were equal. That ruling stood for the next fifty-eight years. Then, in 1968 after numerous uprisings within African American communities, a commission established by the federal government warned that the United States was increasingly becoming two societies: "one black, one white— separate and unequal."

country, there exists a Third World whose exploitation allows the empire to function.

The United States is a white settler nation which came into being with the mass slaughter of the indigenous people of this land, the theft of their land, through the enslavement and unpaid labor of generations of Africans and the terrorizing and lynching of waves of Third World immigrants from the Chinese of the late 1800s to the current immigration of Mexicans and Salvadorans. To this day, race defines every aspect of life in the United States— from the hospitals we are born in, the schools we attend, the buses we

> **The historical development of imperialism alongside the history of European conquest has produced today's imperialist system which is always racist.**

ride, the jobs we work, to our very life expectancy. If we are lucky enough to find work, we toil at minimum wage jobs, multiple shifts and still can't make rent. We live next to the power plants, sewage facilities, chemical plants, smoke stacks, military bases and brown fields required to support the livelihood enjoyed by much of white America. Communities of color have taken the form of internal colonies to be deliberately under-developed and used as mechanisms to accelerate the imperial powers' accumulation of hyper-profits. People of color within the United States have only ever been offered "conditional citizenship" based on whether that group is seen as being supportive of the imperialist powers.[31] Since citizenship is conditional for people of color, the ruling class of the United States can— and history has shown that they do— move to revoke supposedly inalienable rights when it suits them. They did it when they interned more than 120,000 Japanese-Americans in the 1940s, and they do it today by incarcerating and disenfranchising more than 1.2 million African Americans. The enslavement, lynching, legal and extra-legal exclusion of Indigenous, African, Latin American and Asian people from work and wealth within the U.S. closely parallels the experience of

---

[31] These ideas were drawn from the Labor Community Strategy Center's Program Demand Group, *Toward a Program of Resistance,* p. 15.

imperialist domination throughout the Global South.[32]

Another feature of imperialism that distinguishes it from earlier eras of capitalism is the imperialist powers' creation of a 'labor aristocracy.'[33] The dominant position of the imperialist nations allows these nations to extract super-profits. The ruling elite of imperialist nations use some of the super-profits to make significant economic and political concessions to certain sectors of that nation's working class. Through higher wages, greater access to consumer goods and services and expanded social wage such as public education and cultural institutions, the imperialist elite are able to essentially bribe those sections of the working class. In doing so, the imperialist elite create an "alliance between the workers of the given nation and their capitalists against the other countries."[34] For a contemporary example of this, all we have to do is look at the 2004 presidential elections. Statistics show that working class whites in the United States voted overwhelmingly for George W. Bush in an election that could be read as a referendum on the empire's war on the Iraqi people.[35] An analysis that solely focuses on class would suggest that working class whites had and have an interest in opposing a war that, if nothing else, is costing them billions of dollars. But clearly that ain't what happened. Working class whites voted overwhelmingly in support of the war on the Iraqi people. The majority of working class whites, despite their own exploitation, tie their own interests to white supremacy and the dominance of "America" in the world.

The privileges of empire do not extend just to white people (although those privileges do extend further and more frequently). At the same time that our communities are super-exploited, African American, Latino, Asian, Pacific Islander, Arab and Native American

---

[32] Periodically, we use the term 'Third World within' when referring to people of color inside the United States. This term was developed by activists in New York City in 2000. While the term does not capture the real differences that exists in different communities of color inside the empire, it is helpful in making the connection between people of color who live inside the First World and the people of the Global South. Although not identical, it is very similar to the term 'nationally oppressed communities.'

[33] Lenin first introduced this phrase in *Imperialism: The Highest Stage of Capitalism*.

[34] V.I. Lenin, *Lenin's Collected Works,* Vol. 23, p. 114.

[35] Cable News Network exit polling data, Nov. 2, 2004.

people inside the empire gain certain privileges by living inside the empire. One of the most clear examples of this is the level of violence and marginalization heaped upon oppressed nations of the Global South. Clearly, communities of color inside the United States are victimized by the violence of the U.S. government and all of its repressive arms. Without minimizing that reality, it is also true that the U.S. government is much more reluctant— which is not to say that they haven't and won't do it again— to use the full force of its military capacity inside its own borders. This is why we agree with the formulation developed by organizer Eric Mann that the U.S. practices fascism in the Global South, semi-fascism against people of color inside the United States, and bourgeois democracy for white people inside the empire.[36]

Although the level of repression faced by people of color in the United States is not usually as severe as that faced by the people of the Global South, the dynamics are exactly the same. And so is the motivation. All of this is done to allow the imperialist powers to extract super-profits and undermine the sovereignty and rights of oppressed peoples within the United States just as it does from the nations of the Global South. Imperialism would collapse without this level of international and internal super-exploitation— and the necessary repression that comes along with it.

We opened the chapter with words from W.E.B. DuBois. Here, DuBois suggests that the end of imperialism and the emancipation of humanity will only come with the liberation of the working class throughout the Third World, inside and outside the United States. Building off of Marx's insight, he suggests that the forces of change are not simply the working class. Quite the opposite, DuBois shows that the nature of the system has changed, and as a result, the social forces that have an interest in ending the system have also changed.

---

[36] In making this formulation, Mann uses the definition of fascism developed in the 1930s by the then-General Secretary of the Communist International, Georgi Dimitrov. Dimitrov defines fascism as "the open terrorist dictatorship of the most reactionary, most chauvinistic, and imperialistic elements of finance capital." Our assessment is that the policies and materials relations of George W. Bush's government wears different masks in different arenas. While this regime is not an "open terrorist dictatorship" in every respect, it does practice fascism towards the nations and peoples of the Global South. These ideas were taken from Eric Mann's, *The 2004 Elections: A Turning Point for the U.S. Left,* 2004, p. 46.

This analysis represents an important break from assessments of class which suggest that class is simply based on a person's relationship to the means of production. These dogmatic assessments fail to closely analyze the dynamics of the political economy of today's world. They ignore the coronation of the labor aristocracy within the First World. They base their strategy on assessments older than the Emancipation Proclamation. Although DuBois' statement may be non-traditional, because it is based on a more accurate accounting of today's political economy, this assessment helps to accurately explain how the world functions now and offers us clarity about what a truly successful anti-imperialist movement would look like.

U.S. imperialism is based on white supremacy and patriarchy. The system not only exploits workers for the purpose of securing more and more profit, it specifically depends on the exploitation and subjugation of Third World nations around the globe and Third World peoples within the empire, especially women.

To sustain this unstable multi-national system...

To try to address this dilemma and to speed up the realization of profit, the imperialist system developed credit and finance, also known as fictitious capital. Fictitious capital is value in the form of credit, shares, debt, speculation and various forms of paper money. Through stocks, bonds, loans and other forms of fictitious capital, banks lend to businesses the money that they are hoping to realize with the sale of the commodities produced by the working class. Fictitious capital allows the imperialist to launch the next round of production before he has actually sold the commodities from the first round of production. Through credit cards, loans and the like, businesses lend workers the money to purchase commodities they helped produce but don't have the money to buy. Used in these ways, fictitious capital allows the imperialist class to temporarily alleviate the system's inherent and ever-looming crises. Without the assistance of fictitious capital to stimulate the process of consumption, the imperialist system would likely stall because it would be unable to realize the necessary level of profits. Viewed in this way, imperialism is just as much a system of distribution and consumption as it is a system of production.

The cheerleaders and the apologists of the imperialist system claim that this form of political economy is great because of the free market and unbridled competition but, in reality, it is exactly the opposite. There is little competition. Imperialism represents a stage of capitalist development in which virtually all economic activity is dominated by monopolies, companies which have exclusive control over the production or sales of a given commodity.

Imperialism represents a stage in capitalist development where multi-national monopolies are the dominant force in the economy, as opposed to small manufacturers. In *Capital*, Marx observes capitalism's tendency towards centralization. Capitalist production begins with small manufacturers but, over time, larger and more successful manufacturers take over smaller, less successful manufacturers. According to his analysis, this would eventually lead to the creation of monopolies. Marx finishes by predicting that monopolies would eventually become the dominant player in the production of society's goods and services.

In the early stages of the capitalist political economy, the formation of monopolies was virtually impossible because of the limitations of that system. In order for a monopoly to take exclusive control over a particular area of economic activity, they must either buy out or drive out of business all of their competitors. This means that the prospective monopoly must accumulate extreme profits, far more than what is required to simply launch another cycle of production. That monopoly must have enough accumulated profit to launch another cycle of production and to take over their competitor. The capitalist must sell his commodity in order to realize the profit; the ability to become a monopoly depends on having the extremely high rate of sales that would be necessary to accumulate the amount of capital needed to buy out their competitors. In most industries under capitalism, sales simply did not take place fast enough to guarantee the level of capital accumulation necessary to achieve the status of a monopoly. Monopolies became prevalent with the advent of fictitious capital.

With the revolutionizing of transportation technologies in particular, the imperialist political economy has become multi-national. Most imperialist monopolies have spread their production, distribution and consumption activities to different corners of the globe. A good example of this dynamic is illustrated in "Are My Hands Clean?" a song by Sweet Honey in the Rock. The song details the multi-national production and consumption of a shirt sold at a department store in New York City. Before the shirt makes its way to New York, its journey will begin in the "blood-soaked fields of El Salvador" and then return to the United States before heading back to Venezuela, Trinidad and Tobago, South Carolina and finally Haiti where the shirt will be packaged to be sold in New York City.[37]

Globalization pushes the imperialist system to extend its relentless quest for profit all over the globe. However, this process is not happening uniformly all over the globe. Urban centers play a particularly prominent role in the process of imperialist accumulation. Capitalism and imperialism produce cities as much as they produce commodities.[38] Dependent upon the context, cities sometimes serve as production centers (largely in the Global South) and sometimes they are consumption centers (as is the case of cities like New York, London and Rio de Janeiro). But all around the world, cities play the defining role in the development of imperialism. One sign of the increasing importance of urban centers is that more and more people of the world are migrating from the countryside toward cities. In fact, 2005 will mark the first time in the history of humanity that more of the world's population will live in an urban rather than a rural environment.[39] This movement from the country

> **Urban centers play a particularly prominent role in the process of imperialist accumulation. Capitalism and imperialism produce cities as much as they produce commodities.**

---

37 Sweet Honey in the Rock, "Are My Hands Clean?" *Live at Carnegie Hall* CD. 1988.

38 The Bay Area Study Group, "Playground of US Capitalism?: The Political Economy of the San Francisco Bay Area in the 1980s." *Fire in the Hearth: The Radical Politics of Place in America.*

39 Mike Davis, "A Planet of Slums." *New Left Review,* March – April 2004, p. 5.

to the city frequently means a move across national borders to command posts, which are global centers of either production, finance, consumption, or some combination of the three. Cities like New York, London, Beijing and San Francisco have bound their host nations to imperialism's global process of production, distribution and consumption. As imperialism's capacity to produce exceeds humanity's ability to purchase, these global command posts and their local and national governments become even more important as they provide outlets for imperialism's excess productive capacity.

As we established earlier, the imperialist political economy is an advanced and global stage of capitalist development and just like the capitalist system, the imperialist system of political economy struggles to get around the crisis of over-production and the crisis of the tendency of the rate of profit to fall.

The move to more thoroughly connect economies at a global level makes the imperialist system even more vulnerable to plunging into severe crisis. During capitalism's initial stages, if a large bank in England went bankrupt, the impact outside of England would be rather minimal. On the other hand, because the world economy is so fully integrated under imperialism, any disruption in one sector of the economy in any part of the world can have devastating impacts on the global economy. For example, it is now common for large banks to invest millions of dollars in various corporations and development projects all around the world. If that same English bank were forced to declare bankruptcy under imperialism, that action would have ripple implications on local and national economies and could potentially throw the world economy into recession or crash.

The imperialist system is also more fragile because its capacity to produce commodities has far outpaced the imperialist powers' ability to sell those commodities and realize profit. On the one hand, the tools and machines used to produce commodities are more advanced and efficient, which allows the imperialist class to produce more than ever before. On the other hand, the improvement in the means of production means that the imperialist class needs to employ fewer workers. Today's transnational corporations have an incredible capacity to produce, but even with marketing to stimulate consumption by the privileged few, they still get caught up in the poverty they create. All of this makes the imperialist system even more susceptible to plunging into severe crisis. This is why we say that imperialism is an inherently fragile system. On the one hand, the more successful the system is, the more it will blanket the globe. But on the other hand, the more that the system blankets the globe, the more it veers towards severe crisis.

In summary, as the imperialist system inevitably becomes more global, it also becomes more unstable. The imperialist powers employ fictitious capital in a desperate attempt to smooth over the system's built-in crisis. It's stuck in a destructive cycle, prone to crisis, stagnation, growth and inflation— all built upon class exploitation, patriarchy and white supremacy. Under imperialism, monopolies are the driving force of the economy, and their development has allowed the imperialist system to spread itself across a multi-national web of command posts that play a central role in the imperialist realization of profit. This is what is meant by "to sustain this increasingly unstable and multi-national system."

To say that the imperialist political economy is multi-national is not to say that it transcends the nation state, or that the process in some ways transcends the reality of nations. In the imperialist system, states play a vital role in establishing a hospitable or hostile environment for imperialist exploitation. Through tax and domestic policy, trade and foreign policy, nation-states can play a vital role in facilitating or disrupting the process of imperialist accumulation. Whether they exert that power is not the issue. States have a tremendous amount of power and play a central role in helping to sustain the imperialist system.

> *... the imperialist state serves as a manager for global capital.*

Imperialism is an inherently unstable system. Markets do not self-regulate. If it were left on its own, the market system would eventually fall into severe crisis, leaving itself extremely vulnerable. That's where the state comes in. Imperialism needs the imperialist state.[40] Like the manager at a job, the imperialist state has two roles: as the organizer and as the enforcer. In its capacity as manager, the state takes whatever action is necessary, nationally and internationally, to ensure that the system is able to secure the profits it needs to survive.

Through the state, the imperialist powers manipulate their currency's exchange rate. They ensure the privatization of publicly owned resources. They plan military strategies and wage war on other nations to seize control of new markets and eliminate challenges to the system's domination. Sometimes they crack down on other imperialists in order to defend the interests of the system as a whole. The state's actions are always designed to mediate the needs of the system and they change depending on world conditions.

Even though imperialism has changed the way that power is exercised internationally, states in general, and the United States in particular, wield an enormous amount of power. As the leading imperialist state in the world today, the role of the United States is to pave the way for the global imperialist system. With less than 5% of the world's population, this nation has almost complete monopolistic control of weapons of mass destruction, of the world's global financial institutions and of the global communications technologies.[41]

While the United States is the world imperialist super-power, imperialist nations still compete with one another. Frequently the interests of states differ, and all states try to advance their interests. As a prime example of this, France and Germany— both imperialist powers— originally opposed the United States' war on Iraq because the war did not advance their interests. As the leading power, the U.S. needs to balance its national interests with the interests of the international capitalist class. It positions itself as the manager for global capital and is looked to represent the interests of global capital, but at the same time it takes action

---

[40] Jon Liss and David Staples, "New Folks on the Historic Bloc: Worker Centers and Municipal Socialism," 2003.

[41] Samir Amin, *Capitalism in the Age of Globalization: The Management of Contemporary Society*, 1997.

against its rivals in order to stay on top. The war on Iraq is an example of this. The war isn't necessarily being waged in the interests of global capital, but in the interests of a section of the imperialist class based in the United States. By waging the war, this section of the imperialist class gains control of a main supply of the oil used by China and the European Union that they can try to leverage against those nations in the future.

Today it is the United States, as a nation-state, that poses the greatest obstacle to peace and international solidarity in the world. It is not Bechtel that locks up more than two million people. It is not Nike that drops bombs on the people of the world. It is not Disney that rams structural adjustment programs down the throats of governments trying to feed and shelter their citizens. It is the United States and its state apparatus that does these things. As Daniel Ortega, former President of Nicaragua— a nation torn apart by a U.S.-trained and funded civil war, said, "Without the United States, there simply would not have been an armed uprising in our country." Yes, the state is exceedingly powerful. If you have doubts, just ask the people of Palestine, Afghanistan, Venezuela, Haiti, Cuba and Iraq.

The United States was not always the top dog of the imperialist world. Up until the 1930s, the United States was a regional imperialist power within the Americas. Building on the foundation of stolen land and stolen labor, the United States was able to establish an urban-based industrial economy. Then, with the seizure of Puerto Rico, Cuba, the Philippines, Guam and half of Mexico, the United States had positioned itself by the early 1900s as the imperialist super-power of the Americas, but England was still the world's imperialist super-power. That is, until the conclusion of World War II in 1945...

By the end of World War II (WWII), much of Europe and East Asia had been leveled. Like a fox busting into an unguarded hen house, the imperialist forces of the United States moved quickly to consolidate and strengthen their position relative to other imperialist forces. Within months of the conclusion of WWII, the United States had created the United Nations, the International

Monetary Fund and the World Bank. These institutions were created for the purpose of regulating the global political and economic crises. Not surprisingly, not all nations had an equal say in these institutions. Under-developed nations had no voice whatsoever, and as the leading force, the United States gave itself disproportionate decision-making authority in all of these institutions.

It is popular in some circles within the movement today to suggest that the state is no longer important, that states have lost their power. This idea proposes that the real power in the world today rests only with transnational corporations. This view grossly distorts the true nature of what's going on in the world today.

> Today, it is the United States, as a nation-state, that poses the greatest obstacle to peace and international solidarity in the world.

When people within the United States choose to ignore the domination of the U.S. state apparatus, it represents an irresponsibility that is nothing short of criminal.

There is a close relationship between the state and transnational monopolies that is not coincidental. At least nine out of the thirty members of the Bush Administration's Defense Policy Board were connected to companies that were awarded military contracts for $76 billion between 2001 and 2002. Former Secretary of State George Shultz was chairman of the Committee for the Liberation of Iraq, and he also happens to serve on the board of directors of the Bechtel Group. When asked about a conflict of interest in the case of war in Iraq Shultz said, "I don't know that Bechtel would particularly benefit from it. But if there's work to be done, Bechtel is the type of company that could do it. But nobody looks at it as something you benefit from."[42] Since Shultz's comments, the San Francisco-based corporation has received more than $2 billion to rebuild Iraq's infrastructure which the U.S. military has spent billions to destroy. Shultz is far from being the only person with both hands in the cookie jar. Almost half of U.S. Senators are millionaires. As Lenin said, there are thousands of

---

[42] Center for Public Integrity Website, (http://www.publicintegrity.org/report.aspx?aid=91).

threads connecting the state and the imperialist ruling class.[43] These threads are essential to corporations to help them pad their bottom line with money funneled from public coffers. Certainly, corporations wield tremendous power, but it is the apparatus of the state (and during this period in particular the U.S. state) that acts as the manager of the imperialist system.

As people living within the belly of the world's imperial power, we have a responsibility to recognize its brutishness, not to craft clever theories to make ourselves feel better. We have this responsibility because it's only after we come to grips with how and why the United States wields its power that we can challenge the domination of U.S. imperialism, at home and abroad.

This, then, is the fundamental nature of the imperialist system. It is a global system of political economy based on the super-exploitation of whole nations and peoples by the world's imperial powers. To sustain this increasingly unstable and multi-national system, the state apparatus of the United States serves as the enforcer and organizer for the global imperialist system.

As we have discussed, the system of U.S.-led imperialism is more advanced than the system of political economy that Marx analyzed in the 1840s. But Marx's framework is still extremely helpful to us as we try to make sense of the world around us. As we have seen, the imperialist system is prone to crises, creating the conditions that seem to make it vulnerable to change. So that leaves us with the question: What is our assessment of the current state of imperialism? What are today's weaknesses? Where is it going? And who are the constituencies that are positioned to mount a serious challenge to this unsustainable system of exploitation and subjugation?

IMPERIALISM AFTER THE WAR

The post-World War Two (WWII) period marks the defining period in the development of U.S.-led imperialism and the terrain on which we find ourselves today. It was during this period that the

---

[43] V.I. Lenin, *The State and Revolution.*

U.S. became an imperialist superpower. During the three decades between 1945 to 1975, the world political economy experienced tremendous growth; but by the early 1970s, that success became stagnant. Our struggles today are still deeply impacted by this mid-1970s crisis in the global political economy, and the decisions that the global ruling class made to handle it. Understanding the nature of this current crisis, and how it developed, will allow us to develop an effective strategy for justice and self-determination.

World War II was a devastating experience. More than sixty million people died in the fighting. From Europe to Asia, entire nations were leveled from massive bombing campaigns. By the end of the fighting, economies around the world were in shambles. The destruction of the imperialist nations ran so deep that the basic infrastructure of the world community had to be re-assembled.[44]

In the smoldering ashes of atomic bombs and concentration camps, the United States had an opportunity to make profit and strengthen the imperialist political economy.[45] Spurred on by this desire to rake in profit and challenged by the Soviet Union, Third World nations, oppressed nationality and worker struggles, the new imperialist super-power moved to re-shape the fundamental structures of the world's political economy. The political response of the world's imperialist powers was shaped by the reality of the Cold War during which the two global super-powers— the United States and the Soviet Union— jockeyed for world domination. This conflict and competition pushed both super-powers to make alliances and compromises in hopes of gaining ground and

---

[44] It should be said that most of the Global South with the exception of East Asia, the Pacific Islands, North Africa, and the Middle East was not deeply involved in the war. For many of the people of the Global South, the destruction and distraction of WWII gave them a moment of opportunity to try to free themselves from their now weakened colonial occupiers.

[45] But as is the case with all imperialist wars, World War II turned out to be extremely profitable for the imperialist elites. During the war, imperialist corporations were able to produce all sorts of war-related commodities, knowing that warring nations would be in constant need of guns, planes, penicillin, boots, etc. Then following the war, the imperialist powers continued to rake in huge profits in the re-building of the world's infrastructure.

Many corporations got rich during the war and in the re-building process. One example is BMW, the famous car manufacturer. This corporation got its start during World War II in support of Nazi Germany. But instead of making cars, they got rich making engines for German war planes. They were the engine of choice because their engines allowed the German war planes to reach altitudes necessary to bomb English cities.

undermining the other.

CONTAINMENT LIBERALISM & INDUSTRIALIZATION

The political strategy of U.S.-led imperialism in fighting the Cold War came to be known as containment liberalism.[46] This strategy meant that the United States would tolerate progressive economic and social policy within the empire or in allied countries but only if there was an agreement to contain the spread of Communism. Domestically, this was the period when the labor aristocracy was firmly established in the United States. Working class people, in particular white working class people, received higher wages and greater benefits in exchange for the AFL-CIO's active opposition and persecution of Leftists and Communists.[47] Internationally, the imperialist powers of the United States permitted Third World nations to play an active role in the industrialization of their national economies, to carry out land reform, or set up worker protections as long as they did not pursue Communist models of economic development. In a show of courageous self-determination, the Vietnamese people refused to accept these terms, and in response, the United States launched a brutal and illegal war to try to get them to conform.

Economically, the imperialist powers pursued a strategy of massive industrialization. Between 1945 and 1970, three projects fueled post-war growth within the imperialist world: *1) the re-building of Europe; 2) the development of the Keynesian welfare state within the First World; and 3) the industrialization of the Third World.*[48]

> *1.* **The re-building of Europe**— Before WWII, western European nations were responsible for the majority of the

---

[46] Walden Bello, *Dark Victory: The United States and Global Poverty,* 1999.

[47] In addition to the continued exclusion of people of color, the AFL-CIO purged all Communists and anarchists from staff positions in all of its member unions in the 1950s. Thereafter, staff members were required to sign pledges indicating that they were not members of revolutionary organizations. Over the next twenty years, the AFL-CIO played active roles sabotaging the development of leftist trade unions in the Third World. By working closely with the Central Intelligence Agency (CIA), the AFL-CIO had a hand in the murder of trade unionists and in the destruction of workers' organizations throughout Africa, Asia and Latin America. In many progressive and radical circles, the U.S. trade union federation came to be known as the AFL-CIA.

[48] Samir Amin, *Capitalism in the Age of Globalization: The Management of Contemporary Society,* 1997.

world's capitalist production, but the bulk of the war took place on European soil, and by the end of the war, most of the continent was demolished. The imperialist system could not survive if the advanced capitalist nations of Europe were going to be out of the game permanently. To jump-start western Europe's contribution to imperialist production, the imperialist powers, led by the United States, agreed to subsidize corporations to accelerate the re-construction of those nations' capitalist infrastructure.

2. **The development of the welfare state within the First World—** Only ten years before the Second World War began, the global capitalist economy had been crippled by the massive impact of the Great Depression. This global depression threw millions of workers out of work in the U.S. and Europe who took to the streets demanding food, work and relief from the state. The struggles of working people and oppressed nationalities throughout the First World forced the ruling elites to offer certain concessions like public works programs, unemployment insurance and social security. It took the massive military spending of WWII to pull the world economy out of recession, but the First World governments continued social spending after the war. While the social spending might not have been the arrangement that all members of the ruling elite would have chosen, it did serve the imperialist system well. By increasing people's capacity to purchase commodities, and by spending massive amounts of money on domestic infrastructure like roads and highways, the governments helped to spur the growth of the world economy.

3. **The industrialization of the Third World—** Before World War II, large sections of Asia, Africa and Latin America were colonies of First World nations. During that period, the imperialist nations used the Third World as a non-industrialized exporter of raw goods and as an importer of everything manufactured. After having been compelled to fight for other people's freedom in the war, many Third World nations began the struggle for their own national liberation in the 1940s and 1950s. While some of the

national liberation movements fought for socialism and others simply tried to expel their colonial rulers, virtually all of the national liberation movements sought to decrease their dependence on First World's manufacturing and industry. Industrialization then, was a central objective for Third World nations following the Second World War. Although it was by no means universal or complete, many Third World countries did industrialize to some extent in the following twenty-five years; although often at great cost to the environment and people of the countries.

For twenty-five years following the conclusion of World War II, this strategy of containment liberalism and massive industrialization was immensely successful in producing economic growth. In particular, the United States was able to extract a continually rising level of profit, and in doing so supported a rising standard of living for many people living inside the empire.[49] These political and economic strategies contributed to a world economy that was able to radically increase its industrial capacity. From 1945 to 1970, imperialist accumulation grew tremendously.

But by 1970 things had begun to change. Growth had begun to slow down. The European and Japanese economies were re-built and producing. The U.S. economy continued to be strong but the Soviet Union was at its most productive. Plus, more and more Third World nations had developed their economies so that those nations were able to break away from centuries of dependence on the imperialist powers. All of this success brought crisis; there was too much production, too much capacity and too little consumption. The basis of growth for the previous twenty-five years became of the basis for stagnation. The imperialist system's productive capacity, which had brought mind-boggling growth, now brought crippling recession. Areas to invest capital and make a profit were scarce. The global system had reached the point where it was able to produce more than it had the capacity to consume profitably.

---

[49] The economy of the Soviet Union and its aligned nations also experienced tremendous growth during this period. In fact, some Soviet-bloc countries experienced rates of growth that was greater than that experienced by the United States and other capitalist nations. In the case of the Soviet Union, this came at the savage expense of the murder and imprisonment of millions of people under the Stalin regime.

Increasingly, the political assertiveness of the Third World and of oppressed nationality people within the United States threatened to undermine U.S. supremacy. Politically, they had thrown the boot of colonialism from their collective necks. Economically, the industrial development of the Third World meant that Middle Eastern, African, Asian and Latin American nations were no longer forced to rely only on the First World imperialist nations for manufactured goods. Many Third World nations were beginning to band together to adamantly assert their interests, which were often opposed to the interests of the United

> The political assertiveness of the Third World and of oppressed nationality people within the United States threatened to undermine U.S. supremacy.

States and other imperialist powers. To varying degrees, Third World nations could choose whether it was in their interests to produce for themselves, to trade between themselves or to trade with the Soviet Union. This represented a significant loss of market for the imperialist nations. In the United States, the Civil Rights Movement, various Power Movements and the Movement against the Vietnam War, played a similar role. For the racist elites of U.S. imperialism, the ignominy of being challenged by the poor yellow, brown, and black people of Dubois' quote was too much for them to handle.

As a result, the imperialist system fell into widespread recession. Bad turned to crisis-ridden worse for the imperialist political economy in the early 1970s when two events took place that ultimately forced the imperialist powers to adopt new strategies for survival.

At the end of WWII, the imperialist nations had selected the U.S. dollar as the standard currency for global trade when they met at the Bretton Woods Conference in 1945. According to this agreement, the U.S. agreed to link the value of the dollar to the value of the gold in U.S. reserves. But after more than fifteen years of trying to sustain a rising standard of living domestically and simultaneously waging a multi-billion dollar war to contain the spread of Communism, the imperialist elite of the United States had burned through their gold reserve and had literally ran out of money. On April 15, 1971, the United States was forced to break this long-standing agreement and de-link the dollar from the value of its depleted gold reserve.[50] This represented a deep blow to the stability of the imperialist system.

The second blow to the imperialist system came in 1973 when the price of oil skyrocketed. By the early 1970s, all imperialist nations were dependent on oil imported from Third World nations. The United States was consuming more than 33% of the world's oil.[51] Almost all of that oil was imported from the nations of Iran, Iraq and Saudi Arabia who had organized themselves into an international organization called the Organization of Petroleum Exporting Countries (OPEC).[52] In retaliation for the United States' and Western Europe's support of Israel during the October War, the Arab members of OPEC quadrupled the price of oil in 1973.[53] Because the United States and the world imperialist system were so dependent upon imported oil, they had no choice but to pay the increased price.

These two events— the fall of the dollar in 1971 and the oil shock of 1973— pulled the covers back on the crisis of the imperialist system for everyone to see. The world market was glutted with excess productive capacity. The imperialist system had developed

---

[50] In a further blow to the imperialist system, the imperialist elite in the United States de-valued the dollar to avoid soaring inflation a couple of months later.

[51] Wikipedia Website, (http://en.wikipedia.org/wiki/1973_energy_crisis).

[52] "OPEC is an international Organization of eleven developing countries which are heavily reliant on oil revenues as their main source of income. Membership is open to any country which is a substantial net exporter of oil and which shares the ideals of the Organization. The current Members are Algeria, Indonesia, Iran, Iraq, Kuwait, Libya, Nigeria, Qatar, Saudi Arabia, the United Arab Emirates and Venezuela. Since oil revenues are so vital for the economic development of these nations, they aim to bring stability and harmony to the oil market by adjusting their oil output to help ensure a balance between supply and demand. Twice a year, or more frequently if required, the Oil and Energy Ministers of the OPEC Members meet to decide on the Organization's output level, and consider whether any action to adjust output is necessary in the light of recent and anticipated oil market developments. OPEC's eleven members collectively supply about 40 per cent of the world's oil output, and possess more than three-quarters of the world's total proven crude oil reserves." (OPEC Website, http://www.opec.org)

[53] In 1973, Egypt joined Syria in a war on Israel to regain the Palestinian territories lost in 1967. The two Arab states struck unexpectedly on October 6, 1973. For more than three weeks, the Egyptian and Syrian forces defeated the Israeli forces and re-gained the lost territories. But all of this progress came to a crashing halt when the United States funneled massive economic and military assistance to Israel. (Palestine — Home of History Website, http://www.palestinehistory.com/time1900.htm#1973).

the capacity to produce that exceeded its ability to realize profit. Because profits are the fuel of the imperialist political economy, the system was running out of fuel and the global economy was sinking deeper and deeper into recession.

Declining profits meant that imperialism literally couldn't provide the same wages, social benefits and independence that the Third World, workers and oppressed nationalities had struggled for and won. To prevent the imperialist system from a serious crash, the imperialist powers needed a new arrangement. They needed to develop a strategy that would allow the system to extract the necessary profits and maintain growth.

Crisis within the system and class conflict with the Third World forces outside and inside of the empire forced the imperialists to abandon their old strategy of containment liberalism and industrialization. In order to save the world economy from a severe crash, the imperialist powers had to find a way to pump profits into the system. By the late-1970s, new political and economic strategies emerged to become the hope of imperialists everywhere. These strategies are defined largely by three interrelated initiatives: neoliberalism, a casino economy and aggressive militarism.

NEOLIBERALISM

Within the United States, neoliberalism was so universally adopted by the imperialist political elites of both parties that it came to be known as the Washington Consensus.[54] Developed in the 1970s by a group of economists at the University of Chicago, neoliberalism proposes that the imperialist system will be best strengthened by empowering the state to do away with anything and everything that might impede imperialism's ability to extract profit.

---

[54] The Washington Consensus is a term that was first developed by ruling class economist John Williamson to describe the similar policies being advocated by both the Democratic and Republican parties outlining how nations should develop their economies. Williamson summarized the Washington Consensus as a package of the following ten principles: 1) Fiscal discipline; 2) Re-direct public expenditure; 3) Tax reform; 4) Financial liberalization; 5) Adopt a single, competitive exchange rate; 6) Trade liberalization; 7) Eliminate barriers to foreign direct investment; 8) Privatize state-owned enterprises; 9) De-regulate market entry and competition; and 10) Ensure secure property rights. See John Williamson, editor, *Latin American Adjustment: How Much has Happened,* 1990.

In practice, neoliberalism was a complete reversal of the strategy of containment liberalism of the previous period. Though the ten-point package of neoliberalism (listed in the footnotes) came cloaked in seemingly harmless terms, the reality of neoliberalism has been anything but harmless. Fiscal discipline really meant the take back of gains made by Third World nations, women, oppressed nationalities and workers inside and outside the U.S. Re-directing public expenditures meant that the state would offer up what it was taking back to private capital. The overarching mandate of taking whatever means necessary to extract profit furthered the super-exploitation of the working class and in particular Third World women.

The take-back took many different forms. Neoliberal states shredded the social wage of working and low-income people and slashed taxes for the rich and corporations, directing huge sums of money into the pockets of the wealthiest. The privatization of publicly controlled and natural resources, like public education and water, allowed corporations to commodify resources that were once freely available. The elimination of tariffs and the deregulation of financial systems allowed First World corporations to swallow up their smaller rivals in the Third World. All of these measures sought to put resources in the hands of the imperialists and undermine the development of national industries in the Third World. This component of the neoliberal program was vital because these take-backs made up for the profits that the corporations were unable to realize in a period of declining profits.

Another key expression of the take-back has been the soaring debt re-payments from Third World nations to the imperialist powers. Under the guise of offering humanitarian aid, First World nations have extracted hundreds of millions of dollars to temporarily smooth over the world financial crisis. For example, in 2004, the IMF and World Bank offered in $78 million in development projects; during that same year, Third World nations collectively paid $436 million towards debt repayment, most of which went into U.S. banks.[55]

---

[55] "The Impacts of External Debt on Economic, Social and Culture Rights of Nations," 2005 World Festival of Youth and Students, Caracas Venezuela.

However, debt is not solely a problem of finance; its impact is not solely economic. Third World debt is an ideological, political, ethical problem. It is an instrument of extraction of resources from the Third World to the richest nations which greatly undermines the sovereignty of nations. Most of the Third World is paying off debts which were taken on by anti-democratic, corrupt governments, such as the apartheid regime of South Africa. The people of the Third World were never consulted about whether or not they wanted to go into debt in the first place. Secondly, debt re-payment responds to the needs of capital, not to the needs of the people. More often than not, nations are forced to close medical clinics and schools in order to send their payments off to the rich nations. And finally, neither the debt nor the underdevelopment of Third World nations would exist if not for the history of colonization and pillage of these very nations by the imperialist powers. After the United States and other imperialist nations devastated those nation's economies through centuries of slavery, pillaging, trade embargoes and war, the imperial powers are now living off of the wealth extracted from bad loans and high interest rates like loan sharks. The debts are illegitimate. The true debt is historical, ecological and social and it is owed from the North to the South.

> After the United States and other imperialist nations devastated those nation's economies through centuries of slavery, pillaging, trade embargoes and war, the imperial powers are now living, like loan sharks, off of the wealth extracted from bad loans and high interest rates. The debts are illegitimate. The true debt is historical, ecological and social and it is owed from the North to the South.

When countries couldn't pay back the debt, imperialist powers, operating through the apparatus of the IMF and the World Bank, crafted specific packages of neoliberal policies, often referred to as structural adjustment programs. Some packages prioritized the privatization of valuable resources. Others prioritized undermining advances in industrialization. While the rhetoric always suggested that the neoliberal policies were designed to strengthen national economies, the imperialists frequently forced neoliberalism on the countries. One of the earliest and most quintessential examples of the imposition of neoliberal structural adjustment took place in Chile. Here, a U.S.-sponsored coup ousted the democratically elected government of Salvador Allende in 1973. Hundreds of thousands of people were murdered and disappeared so that a military dictatorship could pursue a course of free market fundamentalism and privatization of publicly held assets in that nation. Despite the heinous acts of violence that brought this regime to power (or maybe because of them), Chile became the poster child for future U.S.-directed IMF and World Bank programs throughout the Third World.

For the last thirty years, the imperialist powers have forced neoliberalism down the throats of nations like Mexico, South Korea, Argentina, Haiti, South Africa and all throughout the Global South. Privatization of once-publicly held resources is one of the most common neoliberal initiatives. One example of this occurred when the World Bank forced the Bolivian government to sign a $2.5 billion contract to turn over control of the water in Cochabamba, the nation's third largest city, to the San Francisco-based Bechtel Corporation. Just weeks after taking over the water system, officials at Bechtel tripled the rates for water. Families earning less than $100 per month received bills for as much as $20. Refusing to pay for water, the residents of Cochabamba shut the City down with a series of massive protests calling for the end of privatization. Ultimately, these protests were successful.[56]

Neoliberalism is not just an export to the Third World. Neoliberal ideology has so thoroughly permeated our thinking that most of us don't even think twice about relying on bottled water. Even progressive activists have absolved the state of its responsibility to provide clean, healthy water as a basic right; instead, many of us pay for the commodification of this basic resource. Yes, structural adjustment programs have made themselves at home within the empire too, especially in cities where there are higher concentrations of working class people of color. Privatization

---

[56] Jim Shultz, "World Bank Forced Water Privatization on Cochabamba," Common Dreams News Center Website (http://www.commondreams.org/views/071500-101.htm).

of public education has followed cut-backs to vital services such as women's health programs which have preceded endless tax subsidies to wealthy corporations. Fundamental to the successful implementation of the neoliberal agenda was the role of the imperialist state. Privatization, cuts to the social wage, deregulation and all of the core components of neoliberalism would not be possible without the transformation of the state's role. With the strategy of the previous period of containment liberalism eroded, the welfare state was replaced with the neoliberal state.

Whereas the welfare state regularly intervened to establish regulations governing the process by which corporations attempted to secure profit, the neoliberal state has systematically gone about eliminating virtually all of the regulations that would restrict the behavior of corporations. The aim is to make it as easy as possible for corporations to make profits no matter the social, political or environmental costs. Because the proponents of neoliberalism are so fervently committed to the notion that the market will address all social inequalities— despite the overwhelming evidence— they are increasingly known as free market fundamentalists.

As a result of free market fundamentalism, corporations not only enjoy fewer regulations within nations, but they also face fewer obstacles blocking them from moving some or all of their operations across national borders. Global trade agreements such as the North American Free Trade Agreement (NAFTA) have made it increasingly easy for corporations to pick up entire plants to relocate to a nation with low labor costs and little regulation of the corporations' pursuit of profit.

Free market fundamentalism has also resulted in the loss of power by workers. Take, for example, the re-structuring of work. Increasingly, corporations are producing commodities by sub-contracting or by employing contingent and non-traditional workers. Today, three in ten workers in the United States are working in these re-structured jobs.[57] The proponents of neoliberalism will often argue that re-structured, or flexible, jobs are better for workers, but the reality for most workers is

---

[57] National Alliance for Fair Employment, "Worker Center Strategies: A NAFFE Working Paper," p. 1.

very different. Re-structuring has made institutions that were designed to protect the rights of the working class— such as trade unions and the National Labor Relations Board in the United States— impotent. Corporations are able to circumvent traditional organizing campaigns by moving or denying responsibility.

The core neoliberal principle of driving down the cost of production then turned the imperialists' attention squarely on the Global South. Clearly, the exploitation of Third World nations was happening before the 1970s; as we have previously described, this is one of the defining characteristics of the current imperialist political economy. But in the early 1970s, the imperialist nations stepped it up.

In particular, this quest to lower production costs has led to the super-exploitation of Third World women as workers at home and abroad. The patriarchy of the imperialist system renders women's work invisible and when it is compensated, it is considered supplemental. Corporations have been quick to take advantage of this, recruiting more and more women into the workforce, paying them significantly less than their male counterparts.

The impact of neoliberalism's super-exploitation of Third World women has been a well-documented dramatic increase in the feminization of poverty and low-wage work. Women workers now make up a majority of the global workforce and are an overwhelming majority in key industries like agricultural work, light manufacturing and the service sector.

Women in particular have borne the brunt of the elimination of the social wage, which is the array of services such as income support, childcare, housing aid, health care, and social security which the welfare state provided to supplement the wages paid by the private sector. The loss of the social wage means that workers not only are facing lower wages at work, but fewer social wages at home and in the community. With cuts to these public programs, those costs have been dumped onto the family where it is women who normally shoulder the additional burden. As a result of the loss of the social wage, women around the globe have been forced to enter into the informal economies, including a rising boom in the sex trade, especially in tourist sites and military outposts in Thailand, the Philippines and the United States.[58]

CASINO ECONOMY

The neoliberal agenda advanced by imperialists couldn't completely resolve the crisis apparent in the system. In order to sustain itself the system must constantly expand, this means that capital must constantly be reinvested in hopes of extracting more profit. For capitalists, they either grow or they die. The problem was that during this time, there were few places where capitalists could profitably invest their capital. What they needed was some way to invest their capital that was not tied to the ailing process of commodity production. A solution soon followed.

The mass of floating capital in the hands of the capitalist class desperately needed some outlet for investment, and that outlet came in the form of expansion of the financial sector. A solution was found in what is referred to as "casino capitalism." Developed in the mid-1970s, this form of economy is based on the speculation of currencies, stocks, real estate, etc. Where the capitalists could no longer reliably extract profits by investing in production, they invested in the stock market or speculated in the buying and selling of currency. The deregulation of finance and the move towards a system of floating currencies enabled that process to happen.

The example of currency speculation demonstrates how important the casino economy is to the survival of the imperialist system. Currency speculation is the practice of buying, holding and selling different national currencies to profit from the periodic fluctuations in the values of those currencies.[59] The decision to

---

[58] Many writers including Maria Mies have documented this phenomenon.

[59] Generally regarded as the world's best currency speculator, billionaire philanthropist George Soros is a prime example of the extreme wealth and financial crisis that currency speculation can bring about. Soros came to fame because of his actions on one day, September 22, 1992, when he single-handedly broke the Bank of England. "At the time, West Germany was busy swallowing up the former East Germany, creating a pocket of growth and inflation amidst a European community otherwise marked by high unemployment. As the Bundesbank (the German central bank) moved to raise rates, it threatened the Maastricht Treaty by putting pressure on the European Exchange Rate Mechanism that was to be the vehicle for creating a unified European currency. Even though other European countries needed lower rates to spur growth, they

abandon the gold standard in favor of floating exchange rates in the mid 1970s opened the door for massive currency speculation. When the change took effect in 1975, the ratio of the value of international currency sales to the trade of commodities was about two to one. In other words, twice as much money was spent on currency speculation as was spent to purchase commodities. By the early 1980s, that ratio of currency speculation to commodity trade had jumped to fifteen to one. Today, the ratio is one-hundred and twenty to one. This incredible mass of floating value which totaled 1.3 trillion dollars a day in 1995 moves from one world city to another through electronic transfer.[60]

These developments within the expansion of finance have caused spurts of speculation; notable examples being the Savings & Loans crisis of the 1980s and California's deregulation-inspired 'energy crisis' of 2000. The rise and fall of the dot.com boom and information technology sectors in San Francisco during the late 1990s were a result of the same phenomenon.

All the talk about the "new economy" in reality involves the capitalist class scouring the globe with their capital, hungry for get-rich-quick schemes, investing capital in financial products that often times have at best a tenuous relationship to production. Nevertheless, this circulation of capital has helped to stave off a massive crash of the global economy.

AGGRESSIVE MILITARISM

The imperialist powers knew that in order to implement any strategies to address the crisis, they would need to first de-stabilize Third World forces at home and abroad. Led by the immense apparatus

---

were forced to raise them, or see their currencies decline relative to the powerful German [currency, the] mark. Soros' Quantum Fund [] stepped into this crisis environment to bet against the Italian lire and then the British pound. Indeed, the British position seemed so untenable. Soros [] leveraged an enormous bet of $10 billion. Even as the British government announced a 2% rate hike, Soros kept selling sterling. By evening of that day, the British were forced to rescind the rate increase and withdraw the pound from the ERM altogether. Sterling immediately plunged, [the Bank of England went bankrupt].., and Soros walked away with more than $1 billion in profits. (The Motley Fool Website, http://www.fool.com/Features/1996/spo719c.htm)

[60] International Cooperation for Development and Solidarity Website, (http://www.cidse.org/pubs/cttenapp.htm).

of the U.S. military industrial complex, imperialist forces moved to violently crush any and all opposition. They waged war against the Sandinistas and the Nicaraguan people. They assassinated and illegally locked up freedom fighters from the African American, Native American and Puerto Rican communities. They sponsored coups of democratically elected leaders throughout the Third World. Many of these military operations took place covertly, cautious not to show the true repressive nature of the regime. In the words of Cuban President Fidel Castro, "If there ever was in the history of humanity an enemy who was truly universal, an enemy whose acts and moves trouble the entire world, threaten the entire world, attack the entire world in any way or another, that real and really universal enemy is precisely Yankee imperialism."

Under the leadership of George W. Bush and the reactionary right, the government of the United States has used the War on Terrorism to assume a permanent posture of aggressive militarism. The federal government is developing and purchasing weapons of repression that once would have once only found home on a science fiction movie set, and they are prepared to use them. In 2004, the U.S. government spent more than $455 billion dollars on its military, more than the combined total of the thirty-two next powerful nations.[61] If the meaning of his jingoistic actions were not clear enough, Bush's proclamation of the pre-emptive strike policy has served to put the world on notice: oppose the interests of U.S.-led imperialism, and "we will hunt you down."[62] This increase in the level of aggressive militarism comes as the United States desperately seeks to maintain control of a global situation that is increasingly out of their control.

The impact of the violent de-stabilization of the political and economic infrastructures of Third World nations has created a massive migration of people from the Global South to the First World nations. More people immigrated to the United States between 1990 and 2000 than in any other ten-year period of the nation's history.[63] Corporations in the First World have encouraged this

---

[61] Stockholm International Peace Research Institute, *2005 Annual Yearbook.*

[62] George W. Bush, Address to the Nation, Sept. 11, 2001.

[63] Diane Schmidley, *Profile of the Foreign-Born Population in the United States: 2000.* U.S. Census

flow of undocumented labor-power as these workers have provided much of the hyper-exploited workforce that the corporations have needed. Although they have made it more and more necessary for people to leave their homelands, the neoliberal state has made it less and less feasible to immigrate legally.

While military violence is still the most common tactic used by the imperialist powers to de-stabilize Third World nations, the ruling elite in the United States use a diverse set of tactics. In the last thirty years, they have moved to administratively take the teeth out of the trade union movement as they did in 1980 with the crushing defeat of the Air Traffic Controllers Union. They have also funneled billions of dollars into the expansion of prisons and police forces. In most oppressed nationality communities, parole officers, immigration officials and police act like occupying armies. Today, the United States has more than three million people locked up, most of whom are low-income and people of color. The Black community has been particularly targeted as African American men are six times more likely to be arrested than are white men.[64] For those people fortunate enough to avoid jail, the United States has flooded oppressed nationality communities with untold amounts of legal and illegal drugs to cultivate high rates of substance abuse and alcoholism so that our people would be unable to mount any serious challenge to imperialist hegemony.

All this raises the question, "Has this violence and structural adjustment succeeded in resolving U.S. imperialism's underlying crisis?" In the end, the answer is no. None of these neoliberal approaches have succeeded in resolving U.S.-led imperialism's underlying crisis. U.S.-led imperialism is still a glut of production with few opportunities for productive investment. What neoliberal polices have done is to stabilize a system that has been in crisis for more than thirty years. After thirty years of neoliberal intervention, today the world economy is still struggling with the same crisis.

Bureau, *Current Population Reports, Special Studies No. P23-206,* December 2001 and Randolph Capps, Fix and Passell "The Dispersal of Immigrants in the 1990s" *Brief No. 2* in *Immigrant Families and Workers: Facts and Perspectives.* November 2002.

[64] In a related fact, the United States locks up more people, per capita, than any other nation in the world.

Along with stabilization, neoliberalism has brought tremendous suffering. It has exacerbated the polarization of wealth, it has thrown millions of workers into the uncertainty of contingent work, deepened the feminization of poverty, subjugated Latin America, Asia and the Caribbean while banishing the entire continent of Africa and forcing massive migrations of workers to flee the economic devastation of their homelands. The imperialist elite within the U.S. have attacked immigrant and African American women, smashed and marginalized trade unions, enacted "tax the poor and feed the rich policies" and incarcerated African American and Latino men while funneling huge subsidies for privileged military, computer and bio-technology elites. This impact has been particularly vicious on working class people, people of color, women and the world's natural environment. All of these are being devastated by the imperialists' attempts to save their system of exploitation and pillaging.

The ruling U.S. imperialist elite have been aided in this agenda to re-conquer the world economically and politically by the monopolistic control they enjoy over certain key assets. Among these assets are technology, financial control of world markets, access to natural resources, media and communication outlets and weapons of mass destruction.[65] With this monopolistic control over media outlets and communication technologies, the imperialist powers have saturated the world with deliberate messages that blame the victims of imperialism, in an effort to strengthen the economic and ideological superiority of "a self-selected few, including members of the World Economic Forum, the un-elected leaders of the IMF, World Trade Organization and World Bank; the current imperial president of the United States; and a right-wing majority U.S. Supreme Court."[66] Where they have not been able to convince the people of the world to go along with their exploitation, the United States has used its monopoly over military technologies and weapons of mass destruction to put down any resistance. These monopolies help the U.S. maintain

---

[65] Samir Amin, *Capitalism in the Age of Globalization: The Management of Contemporary Society,* 1997, p. 3–5.

[66] Jon Liss and David Staples, "New Folks on the Historic Bloc: Worker Centers and Municipal Socialism," 2003.

its hegemony and make it possible for the imperialist powers to extract the level of profit needed to stabilize an ailing imperialist system.

U.S.-led imperialism and neoliberalism have also sparked an increased level of resistance, from both the Right and the Left. Massive social movements throughout Latin America, Asia and Africa are contesting U.S.-led imperialism's attempts to stay the neoliberal course. On September 11, 2001 right-wing, Islamic fundamentalist groups, opposed to U.S. imperialism, carried out the deadliest attacks on the United States since the attack on Pearl Harbor. The response to all of this resistance has been more repression. More and more, the empire is resorting to war and violence as a default mode of relating with the rest of the world. This approach is not only costly; it has the potential of eroding U.S. hegemony and authority.

Today, we are living in a particular period of imperialism that has been in crisis since the early 1970s. As the manager of this ailing system, the United States has pursued a set of actions and policies on political and economic fronts in an effort to preserve the imperialist system and to maintain its position of power within that system. These actions become more and more dramatic as the United States faces increasing challenge from the economies of China and India. These changing conditions and the ruling class' actions have changed the terrain on which we struggle for economic, racial and women's justice. The new conditions are undermining the effectiveness of old models of struggle.

hope FRom below

Understanding imperialism and the global stagnation of the past thirty years helps us to see why the imperialists are taking such extreme actions today— it's because they are desperately trying to resuscitate a system which is riddled with internal crisis. However, even though the system is facing critical challenges, imperialism's crises will not be the downfall of the system in and of themselves. The downfall of imperialism will come because of the courageous resistance of those people who have been excluded and exploited.

As Egyptian, political economist Samir Amin says in *Capitalism in the Age of Globalization*, "If the system adopted to manage the crisis cannot survive in the long term, this is not due to the absurdity of its underlying economic and monetary policies, but to the aggravation of social and political conflicts which it cannot avoid."[67]

If the fall of imperialism is to come because of "social and political conflicts," as Amin suggests, the question remains: who will be the leading forces of these conflicts? How someone answers this question is framed by how they understand the nature of imperialism. With a correct analysis, we can identify the sectors of society which have a material interest in advancing an anti-imperialist vision and which are positioned in such a way that they can defeat the opposition of the imperialist powers.

Based on our assessment we believe that the Third World— Asia, Africa, Latin America and the Middle East— must be the leading force of an alliance to defeat U.S.-led imperialism. As the main exploited sector within the global economy, they have a direct and material interest in seeing the complete abolition of imperialism. Their struggle will be facilitated by their greater numbers and their control of the territories which the imperialist nations need for cheap resources and new markets. However, even with

> **Even though the system is facing critical challenges, imperialism's crises will not be the downfall of the system in and of themselves. The downfall of imperialism will come because of the courageous resistance of those people who have been excluded and exploited.**

these factors on their side, the people of the Third World cannot defeat the imperialist forces by themselves because of the United States' monopolistic control over weapons of mass destruction. From the murderous destruction of governments in Mozambique, Nicaragua, Grenada and too many other countries to name, the United States has demonstrated that it is prepared to unleash monstrous violence against any people attempting to challenge

---

[67] Samir Amin, *Capitalism in the Age of Globalization: The Management of Contemporary Society,* 1997.

or step outside the narrow confines of their New World Order. In order to successfully defeat U.S.-led imperialism, the people of the Third World must lead other forces in a broad, anti-imperialist movement.

If the people of the Global South are to lead, this raises the question of what is the role for those of us living and struggling inside the imperialist super-power? What is the role of the two million people locked in U.S. prisons? What is the role of the thirty-two million people living below the poverty line? What is the role Latinos, Native Americans, African Americans, Asians and Pacific Islanders and all other oppressed people inside this racist, sexist and homophobic nation? Simply put, our role is to build a strong movement to address the issues that working class people of color in the United States face that also recognizes that our fights are against the same systems and same enemies as those of the people of the Global South. We play the role of forcing the imperialist states to address the conditions within their borders, as well as around the rest of the world.

Building movement inside the United States poses certain challenges that our comrades in the Global South don't face. Inside the empire, the imperialist powers have saturated large sections of U.S. society with economic concessions and white supremacist ideology in an effort to buy their allegiance. This effort has been successful in a way that makes the building of a majoritarian movement in the United States unlikely. We do not think it is possible to build an anti-imperialist movement in the United States that involves the majority of the U.S. population and that is aligned with the leadership of the people of the Third World. Patriotic racism and imperial privilege are just too deeply held by too many people. But an anti-imperialist movement that is aligned with the interests of the Third World is possible within Third World communities inside the empire. Within our communities, we find enough suffering and discontent to raise a serious threat to the agenda of imperialist militarism and corporate privatization.

To be clear, we are not saying that all of the people in our communities see their fortunes intertwined with those of the people in the Global South. What we are suggesting is that the material conditions for people of color in this racist empire make it possible to build such a movement. The conditions suffered by the vast majority of Black, Latino, Native American, Asian and Pacific Islander communities are more akin to those of the people of the Global South than they are to those enjoyed by the majority of white people in the United States. The very existence of a Third World within the United States is one of the biggest contradictions facing this unstable government.

Although the people of the Global South will play a leading role within the global struggle against U.S.-led imperialism, Third World peoples inside the United States will play an important role too. Working class people of color within the imperialist super-power can, and must, lead a broad anti-imperialist united front which involves people of color from various class positions as well as anti-racist whites. We cannot and should not simply wait for the demands of the Global South to rise to the point of contending for power against U.S. imperialism.

The challenge, then, for those of us inside the United States is to take up those social and political struggles which address the interests of strategic constituencies and which allow forces in the Global South to advance their struggles for self-determination and global justice. What these social and political conflicts look like inside the belly of the beast will be determined by the specific conditions that we are facing. Understanding this leaves us with the question: how does imperialism's ongoing crisis affect the conditions for us here in San Francisco? What have been the responses of San Francisco's ruling elite? And how does all of this shape our struggles for economic, gender and racial justice?

chaptertwo
the 'sco

It's a dog-eat-dog world, you gotta mush on
Some of this land I must own
Outta the city, they want us gone
Tearin down the 'jects creatin plush homes
My circumstance is between Cabrini and Love Jones
Surrounded by hate, yet I love home.

— Common[1]

All of us are working, living and struggling within the context of globalized capitalism. We are faced with a common exploiter and a common enemy. But as organizers, we are also rooted in a particular community which has its own unique history and dynamics. It is for this reason that we must understand and account for the conditions that emerge from this dynamic between the local and the global. Although each local community is closely connected to the same global political economy, each city plays a unique role to keep the system going. Imperialism has a geography. Different cities and regions fit together in the world economy like pieces in a puzzle. The global political-economic system is made up of many smaller pieces that can look very different from one another. Ciudad Juárez looks and functions differently than Buenos Aires. Dar es Salaam is different than Silicon Valley.

It would be really difficult to make sense of each of these economies taken by themselves. Capital and the state organize production, and they bring together in different cities and towns bosses and all kinds of workers to meet their needs. Some cities are centers of industrial production. Others are centers of agriculture. Still others are command posts. All of these distinct pieces come together to form a coherent whole world system. By considering each of the pieces in relation to the big picture, we are able to more accurately understand the role and function of each local piece.

Because of this inter-relationship between local conditions and the larger global system, the changes in the global economy, as well as the developments in a specific regional economy will impact one another. The global system of political economy is a dialectical relationship between the local and the global. In other words, there is a back-and-forth between the global system of U.S.-led imperialism and the political economies of different communities around the world. Each one affects and influences the development of the other.

---

[1] Black Star, "Respiration" featuring Common, *Black Star Are...* CD. Rawkus Records, 2002.

For POWER and our work here in San Francisco, having an understanding of how our city and the Bay Area relate to the global context is an important grounding to our work. We also hope that the example of the San Francisco Bay Area provides the movement with a helpful case study to get a deeper understanding of how the global situation can make itself felt in a city. U.S.-led imperialism exists and impacts people throughout the world, but we all live it and fight it in its specific and local embodiments. By better understanding the context of our experience and community and how they are impacted and shaped by imperialism, we are in a better position to bring about change. So we have to ask ourselves the question in our local context— how does San Francisco relate to the big picture?

In the popular imagination the San Francisco Bay Area is often dismissed as a nearly-socialist state— detached from the political and economic realities of other cities in the United States like Des Moines, Houston or Philadelphia. It is a place where queer people and Left-wingers converge; a place that represents everything that "the heartland of America" is against. Clearly, there are certain qualities that set San Francisco apart. It does have a radical past and is still a place of social progressivism. It is one of the few relatively safe places in the nation for queer and transgender people. It is a place that in that November 2004 election voted for John Kerry, for withdrawing troops from Iraq, and for defending same-sex couples the right to marry, while the majority of the country voted for George Bush and his platform of racist, sexist, homophobic war-mongering.[2]

Even while it often stands apart politically, the Bay Area is filled with contradictions. Even though there is little large-scale manufacturing or production that takes place here, San Francisco is home to some of the largest corporations in the world. While it has been a hot-bed of radical and revolutionary organizations, it has also given rise to notorious right-wing figures such as Condoleezza Rice, William Rehnquist, George Shultz, Casper Weinberger and Ed Meese. Yes, in many ways the City and the Bay

---

[2] San Francisco voted for John Kerry (83%), voted for a local ballot initiative against the war (64%), and marched and rallied heavily in support of gay marriage.

Area are very different than other parts of the world. But beneath all of the hype about being different or out of touch lies a city that is in step with and integral to the imperialists' plans to stabilize and grow their ailing system.

If we were to summarize the most defining feature that is driving the political economy of San Francisco at this time, we would say that...

> *In an attempt to consolidate and expand power in a period of global economic stagnation and rising regional competition, San Francisco's ruling elite has developed an agenda of economic apartheid that threatens to eliminate all of the working class communities of color in the City.*

The same economic stagnation that is affecting the global system of U.S.-led imperialism has put the ruling elite of San Francisco in jeopardy. In response, they have crafted an agenda for how the city can transform itself in order to create openings for expansion in the midst of overall decline. That transformation has come at tremendous expense. The people who have borne the brunt of this massive transformation are working class African American, Latino, Asian and Pacific Islander San Franciscans who have been systematically cast out in the ruling elite's effort to re-invent the City.

The systematic removal of people has been accomplished both with targeted state actions and the removal of legal protections, exposing people to the full brunt of market forces. This has led to the leveling of some of the most vital communities of color in the city and the sharp erosion of space for working class people. It has also meant the removal of the same people whose work built the city and continues to keep it functioning.

As working class people of color have been forced out, corporate industries and a more acceptable (read: richer and whiter) population have moved in. This quest to take back the City has been the thrust of economic development in San Francisco since WWII. It has also set the stage for social struggle in the City. Urban development and removal have been the principal ways that the City has been connected to the global restructuring of the economy since WWII, both in moments of growth and of crisis.

The transformation of San Francisco has not gone on in isolation. It is being carried out by transnational corporations that have a global presence. It is being carried out with money that has been siphoned off from the rest of the world. It is being carried out with methods that are being applied nationally and globally, and often that have been used historically. San Francisco's transformation is intimately connected to the transformation, growth and re-ordering of its immediate region, the San Francisco Bay Area. To talk about the changes in San Francisco outside of the crisis of U.S.-led imperialism robs it of much of its context. To talk about it outside of the context and history of the Bay Area as a region makes no sense at all.

The San Francisco Bay Area is a huge nine-county region that covers about 7,800 square miles in Northern California.[3] It is home to almost seven million people, making it the fourth largest urban area in the United States. From Alameda County and the cities of Oakland, Richmond and Livermore to the east; to San Jose and Silicon Valley in the south; to Marin and Napa in the northern part of the region, the Bay Area is an economic power-house. In fact, if the Bay Area were its own country, it would be the 21st richest country in the world.[4]

The Bay Area is an economically diverse region, and home to a variety of industries: shipping, railroads, petroleum refining, wine production, international construction, government administration, business services, tourism, restaurants, retail, higher education, medical, ship-building, real estate speculation, research and development.[5] Some of these sectors, such as retail, have a lot to do with being a command post in the First World. Other sectors, such as shipping and transportation, have to do

---

3 The nine counties of the Bay Area are Alameda, Contra Costa, Marin, Napa, San Francisco, San Mateo, Santa Clara, Solano and Sonoma. (Bay Area Council Website, http://www.bayareafirst.org/index.html).

4 The Bay Area Study Group, "Playground of US Capitalism?: The Political Economy of the San Francisco Bay Area in the 1980s," p. 6.

5 The Bay Area Study Group, "Playground of US Capitalism?: The Political Economy of the San Francisco Bay Area in the 1980s," 1990.

with being a large population center. Still others, such as tourism, have developed in conjunction with their growth globally. Others, such as wine, tourism, and shipping, have to do the distinct natural attributes of the area. But the global importance of the Bay Area revolves around one key industry: technology. While we recognize the region's economic diversity, we agree with the Bay Area Study Group in their assessment that, "The main engine of expansion in the Bay metropolis for the last thirty years has been the microelectronics industrial complex of Silicon Valley, including semiconductors, computers and instruments."[6]

The Bay Area's role as a research and technology center began during WWII in the context of an arms race with Germany. The Bay Area was a strategic location of arms related research, including aircraft engineering and the development of atomic weapons. From that foundation, the region has grown into an internationally recognized center of research and development for computers, software, pharmaceuticals, biotechnology and nanotechnology.[7] The presence of elite research universities, such as Stanford University and the University of California at Berkeley, have played a key role in allowing this to happen. Bay Area universities produce more PhD scientists and engineers than any other area in United States.[8]

Whereas the U.S. economy overall, and the industrial and manufacturing sectors in particular, have seen jobs and wages decline over the past 30 years, over the same period of time the Bay Area has continued to grow in population and wealth.[9] Last year, the largest two-hundred corporations raked in $66.25 billion, double that of the previous year.[10] This has been possible because

---

[6] The Bay Area Study Group, "Playground of US Capitalism?: The Political Economy of the San Francisco Bay Area in the 1980s," 1990.

[7] "The electronics and biotechnology industries are well represented throughout the Bay Area. With nearly 30% of the worldwide biotechnology labor force and 360 biotech firms, the Bay Area has appropriately been called "Bionic Bay." InfoPlease Website (http://www.infoplease.com/ipa/A0108603.html).

[8] San Francisco Center for Economic Development Website, (http://www.sfced.org/technology.htm).

[9] This phenomenon has been analyzed at length by different authors who talk about the U.S. economy being post-industrial, or Post-Fordist, or changing into a service economy, or information economy, See Jeremy Rifkin's *The End of Work*.

[10] Jenny Straburg, "Profit," *San Francisco Chronicle,* May 6, 2005. (San Francisco Chronicle Website: www.sfgate.com/cgi-bin/topco/home/2005).

the Bay Area has been the hope of global capitalists who have been struggling to overcome the imperialist crisis of excess productive capacity and the lack of productive areas for the investment of capital. The Bay Area has played a key role in the development of global capital's new technologies. The scope and importance of this role has grown and in turn, has driven the development of the economy, the workforce, and the politics of our region.

This role of being the developer of technologies that allow capitalist growth has been exceedingly important, especially in the context of the global economic crisis of the past thirty years. As mentioned previously, all capitalists look to revolutionize the means of production to extract more profit. This search is even more feverish in moments of stagnation or crisis such as we have experienced since the 1970s. The United States not only needs to successfully develop new technologies to find new areas of economic growth, but also to maintain the hegemony that the U.S. empire maintains both technologically and militarily across the globe. As we mentioned earlier, the dominance that the G8 exercise today is built on their monopolization of key assets in the global economy. The Bay Area plays an important role in maintaining and advancing these monopolies in the key areas of research and development and weapons of mass destruction.[11]

The ruling class has funded this project of developing new technologies in proportion to its importance. In an effort to see success, and to speculate and get rich by investing in the next big thing, a constant stream of funds have flowed into the Bay Area through government funding and venture capital. In the late 1980s San Francisco's Montgomery Street — together with Silicon Valley's Sharon Business Center — held the world's largest pool of venture capital.[12] By the late 1990s, 30% of all venture capital invested globally was coming into the Bay Area.[13] Clearly, San Francisco serves as a major investment site for world capital. This steady flow of money into the Bay Area through private investment

[11] Samir Amin, *Capitalism in the Age of Globalization: The Management of Contemporary Society,* 1997.

[12] The Bay Area Study Group, "Playground of US Capitalism?: The Political Economy of the San Francisco Bay Area in the 1980s", in *Fire in the Hearth: The Radical Politics of Place in America,* 1990.

[13] Francine Cavanaugh, A. Mark Liiv, and Adams Wood, directors. *Boom: The Sound of Eviction,* 2002.

and government contracts has been the foundation of the region's growth. It has driven population growth and the expansion of professional jobs and supporting economic sectors.

Today, San Francisco is a command post in the world economy. San Francisco's importance derives largely from the significance of the region, which has grown in importance because of its dominance in the area of technology. Today, the Bay Area stands tall amongst metropolitan regions around the globe.

history by the bay

BIRTH OF A COMMAND POST

For centuries, the land surrounding the San Francisco Bay was home to the Ohlone people. With the sword and the bible, the Spanish conquistadores virtually wiped out the Ohlone people in the 1770s, claiming California in their expansion of colonial Mexico. California remained a part of Mexico until 1848 when the United States decided to seize the territory as a part of its Manifest Destiny plan to complete its own expansion from sea to shining sea.[14] With U.S. victory in the Mexican-American War, San Francisco officially became a part of the United States.

The United States knew from jump just how important San Francisco would be to its rise as a world power. In his State of the Union address in 1848, then-President James Polk commented,

> From its position [California] must command the rich commerce of China, of Asia, of the islands of the Pacific, of western Mexico, of Central America, the South American States, and of the Russian possessions bordering on that ocean. A great emporium will doubtless speedily arise on the Californian coast... The depot of the vast commerce which must exist on the Pacific will probably be at some point on the Bay of San Francisco... The powers of Europe, far removed from the west coast of America... can never

---

[14] Manifest Destiny was the political and religious ideology that the United States used to justify and mobilize support for its conquest and expansion across North America. This ideology suggested that the white race of the United States had a divine mission to expand the country's territory, and God wanted them to do this, no matter what it took.

successfully compete with the United States in the rich and extensive commerce which is opened to us at so much less cost by the acquisition of California.[15]

Situated on the Pacific Ocean and close to immense forests, San Francisco promised to be a valuable asset in the future. Just one year after Polk's address, San Francisco's value jumped, throwing it into the spotlight and setting the course for its contemporary role.

The discovery of gold in 1848 at nearby Sutter's Mill quickly established San Francisco as the urban center of banking, trading, entertainment and supplies for the entire West Coast. In less than two years, this new city literally exploded, growing from a small farming community of just six hundred to a city with a population of 40,000.[16] Even with the gold rush flood of mostly young men, the new ruling class of the West Coast needed more workers to do the heavy labor of building the railroads and other infrastructure that would integrate the West Coast into the rest of the country. They also needed workers to extract the gold that they hoped was "in them hills."[17] In particular, Mexicans and Chileans were brought in to help in the extraction of gold and silver based on the expertise that they had developed during Spanish colonization of the Americas. Chinese workers were brought in to build the railroad system connecting West Coast to the East. The skill and sweat of these immigrant workers created enormous wealth.

Third World workers may have created that wealth, but the white ruling class of San Francisco was going to make sure that they were the only ones that profited. To ensure that the wealth stayed in white hands, Latino and Chinese workers were routinely subjected to deportation, having their land or businesses taken from them, or being attacked by state-sanctioned white supremacist groups. Things got so bad that in 1849 the Chilean government sent a

---

[15] James Polk, "1848 State of the Union Address."

[16] Links to the Past: National Park Service Website, (http://www.cr.nps.gov/seac/earlyday.htm).

[17] Early on, San Francisco's population was 92% male. Most of these were young people who had come West in search of a fortune. More than 200,000 gold-seekers and farmers followed this route to the gold fields and farmlands of California during the 1840s and 1850s. (National Landscape Conservation System Website, http://www.discovernlcs.org/TheNLCS/Trails/index.cfm).

war ship to San Francisco to evacuate its citizens who were being attacked.

Only twenty years after being taken into the United States, San Francisco had become the tenth largest city in the nation. By 1870, with the railroad completed and the hills stripped of gold and silver, the City's white workers felt threatened by competition with the immigrant workers. Immigrant workers in the City and particularly the Chinese community had already been ghettoized and confined to living and doing business in their own community. With most of the hard labor outside the City finished, San Francisco's ruling elite got worried about the non-white competition and set out to white-wash the City, deporting, harassing and terrorizing all people of color. As San Francisco's largest community of color, the Chinese community bore the largest brunt of this attack. Mob violence against the Chinese community in 1877 paved the way for the Chinese Exclusion Act in 1882, which barred all Chinese immigration into the United States.[18]

For the next thirty years, San Francisco solidified its position as command post of the West Coast. It became the financial hub of the region. It was the center of whaling, fishing and shipping, especially with Asia. The region established itself as an educational hub with the founding of the University of California at Berkeley in 1873 and Stanford University in 1891. By the end of the 1800s the economic, cultural and political life of San Francisco was booming. It seemed like there was no limit to how much San Francisco could grow— that is, until 1906.

On April 18th, 1906 an earthquake struck. The 1906 earthquake, and the subsequent fire that burned for three days, leveled San Francisco. Approximately 28,000 buildings were destroyed. More than 600 people were killed. More than 225,000 people were left homeless.[19] The 1906 earthquake was the most destructive natural disaster to ever hit the U.S., and it took the City almost a decade to pick up the pieces. The process of re-building the City served

---

[18] This piece of legislation stayed on the books until 1943. During these sixty years, Chinese immigrants caught coming to the United States were imprisoned on Treasure Island.

[19] SFGov Website, (http://www.sfgov.org/site/visitor_index.asp?id=8087).

to tighten the hold of San Francisco's richest citizens on the City's industry and local government. They were the ones who were most able to ride out the destruction and the ones with the resources to rebuild and expand.

The ruling class of San Francisco did everything that they could over the next forty years to re-build their shining city on a hill, dealing with the Great Depression and a general strike in the 1930s. Their primary success came in establishing San Francisco as a financial center. In this period, prior to WWII, San Francisco became home to the Pacific Stock Exchange and the West Coast Federal Reserve Bank. In addition many large banks, including Bank of America and Wells Fargo, grew up and were headquartered here. Nevertheless, San Francisco still operated in isolation of the rest of the region.

Up until WWII, the individual cities surrounding the Bay like Oakland or Richmond had developed in a more or less independent manner. This created certain problems for the owning class. The haphazardness of this spontaneous organization of business and industry was cutting into profits and into the Bay Area's ability to play its new wartime role efficiently. The completion of the Bay Bridge in 1936 and the Golden Gate Bridge in 1937 had set the stage for the integration of the Bay Area into a regional unit, but the owning class needed an opportunity to re-shape the political economy of the Bay Area. That opportunity presented itself as WWII.

But it wasn't until World War II that San Francisco was pushed towards its current role in the imperialist system. San Francisco's prominence increased dramatically as it became the center of a highly coordinated regional economy, because of the calculated actions of the Bay Area's owning class over the next five years.

METROPOLIS OF THE WEST

WWII was a defining period for the San Francisco Bay Area— just as it was for the United States as a whole. San Francisco became the primary West Coast launching point because much of the war was taking place in the Pacific. Between 1941 and 1945, more than 1.6

million service-men and -women were shipped out to fight from San Francisco.[20]

Seeing an opportunity for patriotic profiteering, several of the Bay Area's largest corporations joined with local politicians and military leaders to form the Metropolitan Defense Committee (MDC). During the war, the MDC took up the coordination of wartime industry and planned defense and emergency services for the region. They eliminated overlap and drafted a clear division of labor for every city throughout the Bay Area. Munitions plants were built in Concord. Research labs were built in Palo Alto and Livermore. And a naval shipyard was built in the Hunters Point neighborhood of San Francisco. By the middle of the war, the MDC had successfully harnessed the entire region into a well-oiled machine designed to support the U.S. war-effort.

All of this activity radically changed the demographics of San Francisco. When WWII erupted, there was a sizable Japanese-American population living in San Francisco's Fillmore district. Based on racist paranoia and without an accusation of guilt, the U.S. government rounded up more than 120,000 Japanese-American citizens and jailed them in concentration camps, claiming that they might be spies or that they might fight on behalf of Japan in the war.[21] When Japanese-Americans were taken away, landlords in the Fillmore district began renting to African Americans who began migrating to San Francisco. During the war, African Americans, who had been largely employed as agricultural workers in the South and had been barred from manufacturing jobs, were recruited to work in war-related industries like ship-building and munitions work. Between 1940 and 1950, the African American population in San Francisco grew ten-fold.

The City also became central location for the gay community during this time, courtesy of the U.S. military. During the war, if a soldier was dishonorably discharged for homosexuality, the military would dump that person off in San Francisco. Instead of returning

---

[20] Economist Magazine Website, (http://economist.com/cities/findStory.cfm?city_id=SF&folder=Facts-History).

[21] This action was taken by Executive Order 9066, issued by Franklin Roosevelt in 1942. In San Francisco, more than 8,000 Japanese-Americans were forcibly removed.

to their hometowns, thousands chose to stay and build community in San Francisco. From that point forward, San Francisco's Gay, Lesbian, Bisexual, and Transgender community was forged much more out of struggle than circumstance. The first gay rights organization in the U.S., the Mattachine Society, was founded in Los Angeles in 1951, but soon moved their headquarters to San Francisco. In 1955, the first Lesbian Rights organization in the U.S., the Daughters of Bilitus, was founded here.[22] The political movement for gay and lesbian rights served as an anchor for the community over time, and San Francisco became popularly thought of as the queer capital of the world. There is a story that is told of a homophobe harassing a gay man in San Francisco saying, "They should round up all you people and put you on an island." The gay man responds, "They have, honey, and you're on it."

> The ruling class was able to transform San Francisco into a global command post and the center of a regional powerhouse. But to make that happen, San Francisco's ruling elite had to wage a series of premeditated attacks on oppressed communities.

The experience of regional cooperation had been lucrative for the Bay Area's ruling elite. Just because the war was over did not mean that they should stop colluding with each other to advance the prominence of the Bay Area as a region. When the war ended, the ruling class kept right on with what they had been doing. First, they moved to re-make the MDC as the Bay Area Council (BAC), a peace-time group charged with integrating the region into a unified political economy. In the BAC's plans for a planned regional economy, each city would play its own particular role. According to the plans, Oakland and the East Bay would be transformed into the hub for heavier industry, chemicals, petroleum refining, shipping and transportation. San Jose and the South Bay would be designated as areas for light manufacturing, electronics and aerospace industry. Contra Costa and San Mateo counties provide auxiliary office space. Because of

---

[22] The legacy of queer rights activism grew tremendously after this period, including the transgender women and queer youth who led the Compton Cafeteria Riot of 1966, the movement to elect Harvey Milk as Supervisor in the 1970s, the strong presence of Act Up (the AIDS Coalition to Unleash Power) and the Lesbian Avengers in San Francisco through the 1980s, and many smaller more recent organizations such as TransAction and Gay Shame.

its history, existing infrastructure and geographic centrality, San Francisco was chosen to be the "center of administration, finance, consulting and entertainment."[23] Connecting it all was the Bay Area Rapid Transit (BART) train system and an elaborate network of highways to link all the sectors of this regional economic system. With plan for regional coordination, the BAC began making their vision a reality.

This would not be a simple task. Even after the war, the region had yet to be integrated into a regional identity. Each city had to be outfitted to play its specific role. Oakland's port needed to be modernized. The South Bay's infrastructure for light manufacturing needed to be expanded. In 1945, San Francisco was not well-suited to play its appointed role at the administrative, financial, consulting and entertainment center of the region. The local economy did not fit perfectly into this vision. Its workforce did not have the skills that would be required. And San Francisco's neighborhoods were not laid out in the way that they would have to be. One thing was very clear; if the BAC's plans were to become a reality, then the ruling elite of the Bay Area would have to transform all of the cities of the Bay Area, especially San Francisco. And that's what they did. After about thirty years, the ruling class was able to transform San Francisco into a global command post and the center of a regional powerhouse. But to make that happen, San Francisco's ruling elite had to wage a series of premeditated attacks on oppressed communities: Rich versus Poor; Developers versus Tenants; White people versus African American, Latino, Asian and Pacific Islander people. Instead of carrying on with the narrative history of San Francisco and the Bay Area, the next section will highlight three case studies, which illustrate the ruling class' relentless attacks throughout this period.

DOWNTOWN V. DOCKWORKERS

Throughout San Francisco's history, Market Street has been the metaphorical— and often geographical— dividing line between rich and poor. At the conclusion of WWII, North of Market was home to the Financial District, Nob Hill and Pacific Heights while South

---

[23] Chester Hartman, *City for Sale: The Transformation of San Francisco,* 2002.

of Market, also known as SOMA, was home for retired dockworkers, sailors, some sections of the Chinese community and the center of San Francisco's Filipino community.

By the 1950s, the capitalist class of San Francisco was in a bind. Business was booming as more and more businesses set up shop in the administrative, financial and entertainment center of the region; so much so that downtown and the Financial District were becoming overcrowded. If San Francisco was going to play its role as the Bay Area's hub, the ruling class had to provide more office space for corporations and businesses.

In many cities, the proposal to expand downtown might not have posed much of a challenge, however the geography of San Francisco presented the ruling class with a particular set of challenges. San Francisco sits on a small plot of land that is surrounded on all sides by either industrialized towns (namely Daly City) or by water (namely the San Francisco Bay and the Pacific Ocean). Every square block of the City is built up in some way, so building out was not an option. And because of the threat of earthquakes, the ruling class was cautious to built up. This means that in order for San Francisco's ruling class to expand the Financial District in the 1950s, they had to tear something else down. This dynamic of the ruling class tearing something down to build something new is a recurring theme in San Francisco politics and the history of social struggle here.

In this case, the ruling class sacrificed the SOMA neighborhood for the sake of the progress of San Francisco's standing in the imperialist economy. The BAC's plans required tearing down blocks of existing housing where people had been living for decades. Tenement hotels and neighborhood centers would be replaced by luxury housing, high-rise office buildings and a convention center. All in the heart of the old South of Market.

San Francisco politicians created the San Francisco Redevelopment Agency (SFRA) to marshal public resources towards the capitalists' development projects. The stated goal of the SFRA was to improve "the environment of the City and [create] better urban living conditions through the removal of blight."[24] Together with the Mayor's Office of Economic Development, the regional office of the Department of Housing and Urban Development (HUD) and large corporations, the SFRA spearheaded the effort to expand the Financial District and destroy the existing community in SOMA.

In the campaign to gentrify SOMA, the ruling elite applied a four step model to displace residents and uproot community institutions and local businesses which included:

1. *Proposing massive redevelopment projects that expand the influence of the local capitalist class and begin the gentrification of working class communities of color.*

2. *Declaring that a targeted community was blighted.*

3. *Using public funds to demolish existing buildings and build new ones for the new corporate residents.*

4. *Taking the area by any means necessary, including the use of eminent domain, re-zoning, tax breaks, etc.[25]*

Working in tandem with the City's daily newspapers, the SFRA so vilified SOMA and its residents that many people saw the Financial District's expansion as a public service. The campaign was so successful for the ruling class that it paved the way for the Financial District continuing to encroach into SOMA over the next twenty years with the development of the Yerba Buena Convention Center and numerous redevelopment projects. Today, you'd be hard pressed to find much evidence that the neighborhood was once the home to San Francisco's Filipino community and the workers who led the 1934 General Strike. The Financial District— its offices and its identity— flows seamlessly across Market Street deep into the heart of SOMA, washing away much of the neighborhood's rich history.

The destruction of SOMA was the ruling elite's first effort to use redevelopment as a tool of displacing people and re-shaping the City's economic terrain. It was the first, but it would be far from the last.

---

[24] San Francisco Redevelopment Agency Website, (http://www.sfgov.org/site/sfra_index.asp).

[25] Eminent domain is the power of the government to seize privately owned property if it is for the 'good of the community.' Under eminent domain, a government can force a homeowner to sell her or his home.

JUSTIN HERMAN V. HARLEM OF THE WEST

African Americans began migrating en masse to San Francisco during 1940s. While there were African Americans in San Francisco long before, WWII brought a massive migration of African Americans from the South looking for work in the war-related industries. Racist renting practices and lending policies channeled African Americans into two neighborhoods: Hunters Point and the Fillmore. Their wages and work built up these communities. In particular, the Fillmore became recognized as the heart of the African American community on the west coast. Musicians like John Coltrane, Billie Holiday and Charlie Parker were regulars in a neighborhood that quickly became known as the Harlem of the West.

The end of the war saw large numbers of African American workers fired from the jobs that they had been recruited into as white soldiers returned home looking for work. Getting no help from racist bosses who refused to hire them and racist unions which refused to admit them, African Americans in San Francisco would spend the next twenty years struggling for an end to discriminatory hiring practices.

By the early 1960s, San Francisco's ruling elite had become proficient at clearing the way for capitalist redevelopment which they now referred to as 'urban renewal.' The new, catchy name was not all that they had on their side. They also had a urban renewal zealot as the head of the Redevelopment Agency. The new head of SFRA was Justin Herman who had previously been the director of the western regional offices of the Housing and Home Finance Agency (the equivalent of today's Housing and Urban Development Department). He began his twelve-year tenure as the head of the SFRA in 1959. His first major project after assuming the post of SFRA director was to put a dagger through the heart of the Fillmore neighborhood.

Quickly, San Francisco's two daily newspapers began running stories on how decrepit and dangerous the Fillmore was. Herman jumped into proclaiming himself the savior of the blighted area. He promised to renew the neighborhood. Herman and the

Redevelopment Agency came up with a development project which called for the creation of a six-lane highway cutting right through the heart of neighborhood.[26] Because many of the Black home owners refused to sell their property, Herman began using eminent domain to force owners to sell their homes and buildings. The Federlein family was one such family. Through eminent domain, they were forced to sell the home that had been in their family for more than ninety years. Once the house was demolished, the SFRA built a parking lot on the property.[27]

Fillmore residents were quick to call things what they were. They saw through all the fancy promises. They said urban renewal was nothing more than Negro removal; and they tagged Justin Herman, "the White Devil." But they didn't just call names, the community organized to protect the neighborhood and defend their land against the Redevelopment Agency's plans. Herman was met with stiff resistance by community organizers like Mary Rogers and Hannibal Williams who were able to stall the project for years. But eventually Herman was able to get the project through. The mini-highway project displaced 6,000 of the 35,000 people living in the Fillmore. But Herman was not finished. In 1966, Herman launched the second phase of urban removal which ultimately displaced another 12,000 people.

When Herman and San Francisco's ruling elite were done with their development projects in the Fillmore, the once vibrant African American community was left in shambles. Not only had thousands of people been displaced but anchor institutions in the community such as barber shops, clubs, churches, grocery stores, etc. had all been put out of business. The community never fully recovered.

TOURISM INDUSTRIES V. THE HOMELESS COMMUNITY

San Franciscans regularly name homelessness as the City's biggest problem. The thing is that people often forget that homelessness in San Francisco was unknown in the 1960s and 1970s. There was poverty in those days, but people sleeping in the streets for lack

---

[26] This six-lane highway is the Fillmore section of Geary Street today.

[27] KQED Television Website, (http://www.pbs.org/kqed/fillmore/learning/time.html#nsv).

of housing was something that you didn't see.

Homelessness emerged as an issue in San Francisco in the late 1970s with the ascendancy of neoliberalism, as the ruling class gutted state-sponsored public benefits, housing and mental health services at the state and federal levels. These cuts caused a sharp increase in poverty and the growth of homelessness nationally. Working class San Franciscans— African Americans, Latinos, and Asians, in particular— found themselves caught in a spiral of rising housing prices, loss of benefits and exclusion from all but the lowest paying jobs. The City of San Francisco opened its first homeless shelters in the early 1980s. By the late 1990s San Francisco had the highest housing prices, the highest eviction rates and the highest per-capita homeless population in the country.

There are now between 7,000 and 15,000 homeless people in the City.[28] Estimates are that approximately 60% of these people were once residents of Bayview.[29] Economic refugees of a system of development that produces a lack of affordable housing and social spending, San Francisco's homeless population is the living and breathing embodiment of the failure of a development model that prioritizes profit over human need.

Homelessness is a major political issue in San Francisco. More than one San Francisco mayor has lost a re-election bid because of his failure to reduce the number of homeless people. This is not only because many rich and middle income people hate poor people (although this fact should not be discounted). Homelessness is a political issue in San Francisco because the City's economy is so dependent on the entertainment and tourism industries.

On the issue of homelessness, it is the entertainment and tourism industries that act as the most reactionary force. They want homelessness and poverty to be erased from the sight of tourists and wealthy professionals to whom they cater their businesses. They don't care if poverty and homelessness are eradicated; they just want it out of sight because their profits depend on the

---

[28] San Francisco Coalition on Homelessness, "Facts about Homelessness," p. 1.

[29] San Francisco Department of Human Services grant application, November 2004.

commodification of the City. According to them, it's simply a question of profits, and homeless people are bad for business.

San Francisco's most activist reactionary forces on the issue of homelessness have been the Golden Gate Restaurant Association and the Hotel Council for the last ten years. Led by these two trade associations, the entertainment and tourism industries have spent the past ten years picking fights over "quality of life" issues, such as eliminating social services or making those services so punitive that no one will access them.[30] In 2002, the Golden Gate Restaurant Association, in partnership with then-mayoral candidate Gavin Newsom, sponsored a ballot proposition to cut public benefits to homeless people. It was the third attempt to slash welfare benefits in five years. Pouring almost a million dollars into the campaign, the entertainment and tourism industries' Care Not Cash initiative served as a rallying point for people frustrated with the City's failed homeless policies.

MANHATTAN OF THE BAY

As each of the three case studies illustrated, San Francisco's ruling elite have been advancing a plan that they crafted fifty years ago. A central part of that plan was transforming all of the Bay Area into the major metropolitan region of the West Coast. They wanted the Bay Area to be the New York of the West. They wanted to coordinate the region's political economy into a coherent and powerful entity that vaulted their position in the global pecking order. Like each of New York's five boroughs plays a different role in the City's political economy, the ruling class of the Bay Area assigned different cities different roles.

It was always clear that San Francisco would have to be the center of this constructed regional economy. As the former President of BART's Board of Directors said in 1968, "It's not a question of whether it's desirable. It's the only practical way. Certain finance, banking industries, want to be centralized, want to have everyone near each other... There's also a cultural aspect. You can't have the

---

30 "Quality of life" is a term used by forces in San Francisco who support the removal of poor or homeless San Franciscans, the cutting of social services, and in particular more police intervention to get poor people out of public spaces. The quality of life they are talking about is that of yuppies who don't want contact with poor people.

symphony, the opera, the ballpark in every community." Reading the words of another BART official, Roger Lapham, Jr., it is also clear that San Francisco was always going to be the center: "The end result is that San Francisco will be just like Manhattan."[31]

Comparing both cities makes it obvious just how successful the ruling class has been. Compared to the Bronx, Brooklyn, Queens and Staten Island, Manhattan is the main center of luxury housing, retail consumption, restaurants, tourism, finance and business, culture and entertainment. Manhattan is home to the famous New York skyline, Central Park, Grand Central Station, Radio City Music Hall, Broadway, Soho, Chelsea, Mid-town, the Upper-West Side, the Museum of Natural History. It's where New York University and Columbia University are. The Macy's Day Parade. The Oak Room at the Plaza Hotel. It's the place that gives the word cosmopolitan its meaning. Manhattan is urban, wealthy, and cultured.

In the Bay Area, San Francisco is where transnational corporations base their headquarters, right next to hot-shot law firms, brokerage houses and marketing firms. San Francisco is home to the Pacific Stock Exchange, the regional branch of the Federal Reserve Bank, Charles Schwab and Bechtel. It is where you find the Chinese New Year Parade and LGBT Pride, four major art museums, the Opera, and several smaller theaters and galleries. It is the center of government administration for the region, the place with state and federal offices and international embassies. It is also the site of luxury housing, fancy restaurants, five-star hotels and world-class shopping— the city of cable cars, Union Square, Lombard Street, Fisherman's Wharf, the Presidio, Candlestick Park, and the Tonga Room of the Fairmont Hotel. San Francisco is the enclave for the young, professional, fashionable, and wealthy to have trendy, artsy, big city living.

None of this wealth has come without consequences. All of this so-called progress has come at the direct expense of working class communities of color, but as the elites of the world would say, "You can't make an omelet without breaking a few eggs." To get

---

[31] *San Francisco Bay Guardian News,* October 18, 2000. San Francisco Bay Guardian Website, (http://www.sfbg.com/News/35/03/03chron.html).

from "Gangs of New York" to "Breakfast at Tiffany's" you have to make some significant changes. Manhattan is increasingly where Chinese, African Americans, Puerto Ricans, Dominicans, Haitians and Africans are not. Neighborhoods whose names have, for decades, been synonymous with communities of color are being gentrified and whitened. Manhattan is less and less where you find a Puerto Rican Lower East Side or Barrio, a Chinese Chinatown, a Dominican Washington Heights or an African American Harlem. Increasingly, it's the borough within the city of New York where business people, the white and the wealthy come together to live, work and play while they are served by working class people of color who must leave on the train once their shift is over.

The same has been true in San Francisco. In the last thirty years, San Francisco is less and less home to a transgender Tenderloin, an African American Fillmore, a Filipino Manilatown,

> The imperialist elite turned San Francisco into the Madonna of the global command posts. Madonna's role within the music industry and pop culture is to be on the cutting edge, always one step ahead. From "Lucky Star" to her current fascination with techno, the Material Girl has made a career of re-inventing herself. That, too, is San Francisco's role.

a Latino Mission, a African American Bayview or a Chinese Chinatown. Drunk with their class' success, real estate developers and brokers have gone so far as to trash the old and blighted names of the communities. Manilatown has all but disappeared. The Tenderloin has been re-discovered as Lower Nob Hill, and Bayview Hunters Points is being called Bayview Heights. Although African American, Latino and Asian communities do remain in San Francisco, the ruling class is waging a vicious displacement campaign so that they can further expand their privileged position as a command post of U.S.-led imperialism.

madonna in the 'sco

As you approach the mayor's office in San Francisco's City Hall, after you've made it past the metal detectors and armed guards, you see the busts of two former mayors. One is of Diane Feinstein.[32] The other is of George Moscone.[33] Underneath Moscone's bust there's a quotation that reads:

> *San Francisco is an extraordinary city because its people have learned how to live together with one another, to respect each other and to work with each other for the future of their community. That's the strength and the beauty of this city— and it's the reason why the citizens who live here are the luckiest people in the world.*

Moscone's words capture the beatific image that many of San Francisco's ruling elite have of their shining city on a hill—tolerant, caring, respectful of difference and community-minded. But this idyllic image is the exact opposite of the lived experiences of working class people of color who have been cast out of the city so that San Francisco's ruling elite could consolidate and expand their privilege.

At untold costs, the ruling class has solidly established San Francisco as the hub of the Bay Area's regional economy. This did not come about naturally. Over the last fifty years, the ruling class has conspired to mold San Francisco's political economy so that it would best serve their interests and the interests of global capital. Their deliberate policies and actions have affected San Francisco in a myriad of ways. The City's economy is organized and managed to be able to fill that role. New development projects are evaluated on the basis of whether they will help the City play its role. All of this has had, and continues to have, a profound impact on the social and economic landscape of the City. It shapes what industries are now located here, who works here and who lives here.

---

[32] Diane Feinstein was a member of the San Francisco Board of Supervisors in the 1970s. After the assassination of Mayor George Moscone and Supervisor Harvey Milk, Feinstein was appointed as Mayor, and went on to hold the office for the next 10 years. She is married to Richard Blum, a powerful investment banker. Many people mark her time as mayor as a shift toward a more business-centered politic in San Francisco city government. She has gone on to hold several terms on the U.S. Senate.

[33] George Moscone was one of the most progressive mayors in San Francisco's history. His life was cut short in a homophobic anti-civil rights backlash, when conservative supervisor Dan White broke into his office and assassinated Moscone and Supervisor Harvey Milk, the first openly gay elected official in the U.S. and a crusader for queer rights and civil rights.

San Francisco is often referred to as the quintessential post-Fordist city because it is a city that for years has grown more and more wealthy despite the fact that there is no traditional manufacturing industry that takes place here. Whereas São Paulo builds cars, Beijing sews clothing and Silicon Valley assembles computers, that is not the role that San Francisco's designed to play. San Francisco's role was, and continues to be to revolutionize the means of production for the world system of production.

In essence, the imperialist elite turned San Francisco into the Madonna of the global command posts. Madonna's role within the music industry and pop culture is to be on the cutting edge, always one step ahead. From "Lucky Star" to her current fascination with techno, the Material Girl has made a career of re-inventing herself. That, too, is San Francisco's role. Whether it is the development of personal computers, the commercial utility of the internet, or advances in biotechnology, the imperialists rely on San Francisco to help fulfill one of capitalism's most basic needs. Other cities can build stuff, sew stuff and assemble stuff. Within the global political economy, San Francisco is responsible for coming up with— or at least funding Silicon Valley to come up with— the next big thing.

San Francisco's local economy revolves around four key industries: finance, technology, real estate and entertainment/tourism. These Big Four Industries are not only central figures in San Francisco's economy, they also represent some of the most influential movers-and-shakers in local politics.[34]

Linked to the Big Four Industries is the service sector. The service sector is a multi-tiered sector of the economy; some aspects, such as law firms and marketing firms, are high-wage and high-profile, but the overwhelming majority of San Francisco's service sector is classified as low-wage work. Although the bulk of service work is low-waged and under-appreciated, that is not to say

---

[34] San Francisco ruling class politics today are run by the Big Four: real estate speculators (like Shorenstein, the Residential Builders Associations), the tourism industry (like the Hotel Council, the Golden Gate Restaurant Association, Union Square Business Improvement District), technology (UCSF, dot-com start-ups) and the downtown business elites (the Committee on Jobs, SF Chamber of Commerce)[6]. These are the business groups that represent the dominant economic sectors of the city, and shape many of the economic development policies of the city.

that it is superfluous. San Francisco's service sector ensures the reproduction of the Big Four, in the same way women's work in the household reproduces the working class. Workers at Kinko's allows law firms to distribute legal briefs to those who need them. Bicycle messengers quickly deliver architects drawings. And nannies and coffee vendors make it possible for stock brokers to work twelve-hour days. Without industries that catered to the specific needs of the industries and their employees, the Big Four would drown in a pool of inefficiency. In a general sense, San Francisco's economy resembles an hour-glass. There are a lot of jobs on the top and the bottom which are connected to one another by a skinny middle strata.

This over-emphasis on professional and technocratic jobs has helped to cultivate a wealthy and educated populace. In 2000, San Francisco had the third highest average household income in the country (behind San Jose and Anchorage).[35] Today, more than 50% of San Franciscans have a college degree which makes the City the fourth most educated city in the country.[36] Over the last decade, the percentage of San Francisco residents with at least a bachelor's degree increased by 47% while the percentage with less than a high school degree fell by 23%. But one quick look at the following statistics shows us that although San Francisco on the whole is wealthy, the rising tide of capitalist progress has not lifted all boats equally.[37]

	Number of Residents	% of SF Population	Per Capita Income
White	385,728	49%	$48,393 a year
Asian	239,565	31%	$22,357 a year
Latino	109,504	14%	$18,584 a year
African American	60,515	8%	$19,275 a year

In a not-so shocking turn of events, San Francisco's workforce is highly racialized. Over the past decade per capita income in the

35 U.S. Census Bureau, 2003 American Community Survey: Ranking Table 2003, Median Household Income.

36 Cities were ranked by the percent of the population aged 25 years and over with a college or professional degree.. CensusScope Website, (http://www.censusscope.org).

37 For population statistics, refer to SFGov Website, http://www.sfgov.org/site/bdsupvrs_page.asp?id=4783). For per-capita income statistics, see the American Fact Finder: US Census Bureau.

city increased 30% and household income increased 40%.[38] Of course, it is not that everyone is getting richer; it's that low-wage workers, particularly African American, Latino and Asian workers, are being forced out of the City.

But even as they are forced to leave, working class people of color still come back into the City to work, largely in the low-wage end of the service sector. Today's new service sector workers who are predominantly Latin American and Asian immigrants, face low pay, little or no benefits, under-employment, unstable work and often hazardous conditions. Many of these immigrants working in the low-wage service sector are forced to triple up in apartments so that they can afford the sky-rocketing rents or else they pay the costs of commuting. Although these workers play a vital role sustaining San Francisco's economy, the state has subjected immigrant workers to incredible abuse. For example, since late 2001 immigrant workers have been subject to increased anti-immigrant attacks, and the City has largely stood by as the Immigration and Naturalization Services (INS) has stepped up its raids of the Asian and Latino communities. All in keeping with San Francisco's long track-record of racist abuse of working class people of color.

Not only is San Francisco's service sector highly racialized, it is also highly gendered. Women workers play a central role in several key industries in the service sector. As janitors, waitresses, hotel workers, laundry cleaners, domestics, child care workers, home-care workers and sex workers— all jobs that are highly gendered, women workers provide critical service to the functioning of San Francisco's Big Four Industries.

Since the closure of the Navy's shipyard in 1974 and the neoliberal cut-back of the public sector, San Francisco's ruling elite have systematically relegated the African American community to the reserve army of labor. The official rate of unemployment in San Francisco is 4.5%.[39] In the Black community, the official unemployment rate is 11.4% but estimates are that the

---

[38] SFGov Website, (http://www.sfgov.org/site/bdsupvrs_page.asp?id=4783).

[39] California Employment Development Department, "Monthly Labor Force Data for Counties," December 2004.

unemployment is really much closer to 50%. This exclusion from jobs and the soaring costs of living have forced thousands of African Americans to flee the City. Over the past ten years, the African American population has dropped by more than 23%.[40] But it's not just individuals who are leaving. Anchor institutions such as Black-owned businesses and churches, unable to secure loans because of banks' red-lining practices, have been victims of gentrification as well. Those African Americans who have remained in the City have borne the brunt of police brutality and have been targeted to fill the ever-expanding prison industrial complex.

San Francisco has the highest percentage of gay men in the United States, and the Castro continues to be the center of much of San Francisco's gay community. However, in recent years, the Castro has become more and more white and more and more affluent. In line with this transformation, the image of queer people in the City is portrayed as a young, professional, white, gay man. However, in reality, there are multiple queer communities in the City by the Bay. San Francisco's lesbian, gay, bisexual, and transgender communities are much more multi-class and multi-racial than the popular image would acknowledge. Low-income African American, Latino, Asian, and Pacific Islander queer San Franciscans, especially women, are increasingly being pushed into the poorer, more multiracial and transgender Tenderloin, or out of the City altogether. As a result of this outward migration, Oakland recently surpassed San Francisco with the highest population of queer women in the country.

Yes, the ruling elite have left their mark. Under their careful and relentless management, San Francisco has become the Madonna of the global command posts, outfitted with a matching economy, workforce and population. In the process, the ruling elite had to make San Francisco less working class, less queer, and much less African American, Latino, Asian and Pacific Islander than it was fifty years ago. All the while, San Francisco's largest corporations continue to gorge themselves on profits, extracted from the exploitation of a workforce that is overwhelmingly low-income,

---

[40] SFGov Website, (http://www.sfgov.org/site/bdsupvrs_page.asp?id=4783).

female, immigrant, of color.

Many people might argue that these communities have been so ravaged by the last fifty years of displacement and gentrification that the future of San Francisco is a foregone conclusion. That it is only a matter of time before the ruling class completes their project of making all of San Francisco an exclusive playground for wealthy and white professionals and technocrats. We don't think that the fight is over just yet, but the struggle for self-determination in San Francisco's working class communities of color is at a tipping point. If the ruling class is allowed to advance their agenda in the next few years, African American, Latino, Asian and Pacific Islander communities will not have the strength or positioning to mount a successful counter-offensive. The time is now for a campaign to protect vibrant working class communities in San Francisco, but any successful campaign will need to be rooted in a sharp understanding of the ruling elite's agenda and their tactical plan.

THEIR SCHEMES, OUR LIVES

Despite all of their success over the past fifty years, San Francisco's ruling elite is not content because they are staring at a series of grave challenges. These challenges are putting the ruling elite's privileged status within the imperialist order in jeopardy. Desperate not only to consolidate but also expand their privilege, the pro-imperialist politicians and leaders of San Francisco's largest corporations have developed a clear agenda for the future development of the City. The implementation of this tactical plan would spell the demise of all working class communities of color in San Francisco.

The challenges are coming from both the global and regional levels. As we discussed in chapter one, the global imperialist system is currently tangled up in its own crisis. The imperialist system has developed an excess of productive capacity. The result is that the imperialists are capable of producing more commodities than society can profitably consume. If the system is run at full-speed, a crisis of over-production will ensue. But holding back from running the system at its peak capacity means that there are fewer places where the imperialists can profitably invest their capital. Especially since the collapse of the dot.com bubble in the 1990s, the imperialists have chosen to hold back and investors have been reluctant to float capital. As one of the global command posts charged with managing the flow of financial capital, San Francisco has been deeply impacted by this crisis of the imperialist system.

The other challenge is coming from other cities and regions, each jockeying to take over San Francisco's role. San Francisco is in constant competition within the Bay Area, the nation and the world to maintain and expand its position. As one example, there is an on-going rivalry between San Jose, the technology center, and San Francisco, the business and finance center. Each city is constantly vying to snatch parts of the other's economic base. San Francisco has repeatedly tried in past decades to attract some of the Bay Area's research and technology work, as was the case with the dot.com businesses and the current plans to develop a biotech industrial complex. The challenges are not just from other Bay Area cities. The city of Los Angeles, and its broader metropolitan region which includes San Diego, poses a serious threat to the ruling elite of San Francisco, and the Bay Area, in both the financial and technology industries.

So despite all of their success, San Francisco's ruling elite is not comfortable. In response to the looming challenges, San Francisco's Big Four have developed an agenda of the changes they want to see happen so that they can strengthen their ability to extract wealth. Simply put, they want San Francisco's public and private sectors to support development projects which will create three things: *1) market-rate housing, 2) white-collar jobs and 3) low-wage service sector jobs.* This agenda they believe will solidify San Francisco's role within the imperialist order, at least for the time being.

To advance their agenda, the Big Four has a tactical plan that borrows heavily from the four-step process applied by the Redevelopment Agency. In order to carry out their agenda, the

Big Four had to establish support within city government. City government is critical to the Big Four's plans because, the corporate elites don't want to have to foot the bill, especially during a period of potential recession. In keeping with the neoliberal model, the ruling elite want to use public resources to pay for their privately controlled ventures. Additionally, the Big Four will look to their governmental partners to relax regulations which could slow the development of these projects.

It doesn't take much to see how successfully the Big Four have organized support for their agenda within the highest levels of San Francisco's city government. In his campaign materials from 2002, San Francisco Mayor Gavin Newsom called on local government to "place priority on development projects" and "to streamline regulations and meet accelerated schedules for approving worthy new public and private projects."[41] In other words, Newsom sees the role of government as making San Francisco safe for capitalism. The thousands of strings connecting the capitalist class to City Hall are so strong that not only are their interests the same but so is their language. Mayor Newsom describes himself as the CEO of San Francisco and says "the City is my Client." With all of their pieces in place, San Francisco's ruling elite have already begun rolling out the same four-step process used by the City's Redevelopment Agency during the urban removal projects of the 1950s and 1960s (for a description of the four-step process, refer to the "Downtown v. Dockworkers" section on page 91).

The first step of this plan, then and now, is to propose massive redevelopment projects that would expand the influence of the local capitalist class and begin the gentrification of working class communities of color. San Francisco's Redevelopment Agency and Planning Department are looking to move more than thirty different development projects forward.[42] The center piece of the ruling elite's development plans is Mission Bay. The Mission Bay

---

[41] Mayor Gavin Newsom Website, (http://www.gavinnewsom.com/index.php?id=27).

[42] See the "Pressures Map" from There Goes The Neighborhood, POWER's demographic survey of the Eastern neighborhoods. There are also a variety of documents available currently on the internet on the websites of the chamber of commerce, and other groups that lay out their goals and plans. For more examples, see http://www.sfchamber.com/sf_plans_2020.htm, http://www.sfchamber.com/, http://www.sfced.org/, http://www.ggra.org/html/hot_issues.cfm.

Project seeks to develop a "new neighborhood" by constructing, in partnership with the University of California-San Francisco, a gigantic biotech research and development complex. This is the only proposal of the thirty that would bring new production in the City. However, the jobs created by the Mission Bay project would, almost exclusively, be for highly-educated, highly trained professionals. The hand full of entry-level jobs that this project would create are likely to be janitorial or very low-wage work in the production side of biotechnology, offering no real opportunity for advancement.

Taken together, these thirty development projects would create a windfall of market-rate housing development. The twelve development projects highlighted in the Mayor's proposals alone would create 15,690 units of market-rate housing and only approximately 1,200 units of low-income housing.[43] Eighteen of the new development projects create retail or commercial space. In short, these projects focus on consolidating and expanding San Francisco's current role as a center of tourism, entertainment, luxury consumption, upscale housing, financial and business services, and the new growth sector of biotechnology. On the other hand, these projects would do little to meet low-income San Franciscans' need for stable community, affordable housing and accessible jobs that pay a livable wage.[44]

Having crafted proposals for massive development projects, San Francisco's ruling elite are now actively engaged in trying to carry out the second and third steps. The second step is to declare a community full of blight. In the 1950s, the City's newspapers,

---

[43] Zoning requirements mandate a certain percentage of new housing developments must be designated for low-income tenants. New developments on the city's polluted brownfield sites are slated to have a higher concentration of low-income housing ("almost one third" of 1600 in Hunters Point Shipyard, and 30-50% of 750 at Shlage Lock development in Visitation Valley). Waterfront, city-subsidized private developments such as Rincon Hill and the Transbay Terminal tend to only meet the minimal requirements of affordable housing, or even attempt to locate the low-income housing "off-site" in a different neighborhood all together.

[44] Beyond that, there are projects of transportation or land reclamation (in particular environmentally). The projects detailed in "Building a Strong Local Economy" are not the entirety of the projects that are on tap. In addition there are other urban renewal projects such as: Halliday Plaza, the Mint Building, a 30th Street BART station, a 16th Street Lightrail, the Third Street Corridor and Central Subway, the destruction of the Hunters Point housing projects in Middle-Point, Harbor Road, and Double Rock, and several proposed Redevelopment zones throughout the Eastern Neighborhoods.

business leaders and politicians all began singing the chorus about the need to 'clean up' the blight of the Fillmore. Today, the City's one daily newspaper, business leaders and politicians have begun calling for the City to be cleaned up. The most notable instance has been with Bayview/Hunter's Point. The City is targeting the last strong African American neighborhood left in San Francisco for redevelopment and urban removal. After decades of economic isolation, toxic contamination and some of the highest cancer and asthma rates in the country, the City is not stepping in to address any of the real demands the community has been fighting for over the last thirty years. Instead, the City is trying to take advantage of the conditions that our communities have endured, claiming the need to tear down the neighborhood in order to save it. Alongside plans for condo-conversion and mini-malls, the City is suddenly interested in cleaning up the environmental catastrophe created by the Navy and Pacific Gas and Electric (PG&E) so many decades ago.

The third step in the four-step process is to secure public funds to demolish existing buildings and build new ones for the new corporate residents. Although the ruling elite have yet to launch their full-blown campaign to grab as much public funds as possible, local politicians have started the corporate welfare programs. In 2004, San Francisco's Board of Supervisors approved a ten-year exemption to the City's 1.5% pay-roll tax for all biotech companies that located in San Francisco. The Redevelopment Agency has also served as a tool for the elite for siphoning public money to subsidize private corporations. In the last few years alone, the Redevelopment Agency gave $27 million to Bloomingdale's to build their new department store downtown, $71 million to subsidize the construction of the new Mission Bay biotechnology complex and subsidized several other private development projects.[45]

In addition to the tax breaks and public subsidies, the ruling elite will be looking to circumvent as many City regulations as possible. In recent years, state policies and protections around rent control, housing construction and condo conversion have been key arenas

---

45 The Building and Construction Trades Council of San Francisco Website, (http://www.sfbctc.org/82503-construction.htm).

of struggle for working class people of color in San Francisco. Attempts to streamline parts of the Planning Commission process and to limit or remove rent control have met broad-based opposition. The City's real estate developers and speculators want a free hand to build and sell whatever the market will support. They want to abolish the planning processes, construction regulations, tenant and community protections because of the impact that this type of legislation has on the market's ability to extract profit. This is neoliberalism, pure and simple, and judging from his campaign materials, it seems that the Mayor will be extremely supportive of any attempt to streamline regulations.

The final step is to take the area by any means necessary. This stage of the present struggle has yet to fully develop, but it is only a matter of time. Today, the San Francisco Redevelopment Agency has development plans for the next thirty years which cover most areas of the City. For example, the City's is projecting that with the adoption of their plans one out of every four new arrivals to San Francisco in the next twenty-five years will move into Bayview Hunters Point.[46] The fact of the matter is that the housing does not exist to accommodate this influx. To make way, the ruling elite will have to displace the current residents in Bayview, and they won't stop there. The City's ruling elites are desperate to snatch up many of the working class communities so that they can attract new industries and make up for the disintegration of the dot.com industry. To this, they have targeted eight working class communities which they have now labeled the "Eastern Neighborhoods"— Chinatown, the Tenderloin, South of Market, the Mission, Excelsior, Potrero Hill, Bayview Hunter's Point, and Visitation Valley— the neighborhoods which have historically been home to San Francisco's largest communities of color.[47]

---

[46] Draft Environment Impact Report for "Bayview Hunters Point Redevelopment and Zoning" prepared by the San Francisco Redevelopment Agency and San Francisco Planning Department, October 19, 2004, page S-8. The Environmental Impact Report states that the project area plan anticipates a population growth of 20,896 by 2025, and "would account for nearly one-quarter (24 percent) of the citywide population growth (80,100 residents) anticipated in San Francisco during this same 25-year period." Without the adoption of the Redevelopment Plan, the anticipated population growth in Bayview is only 2,815 new residents by 2025.

[47] For more information on the neighborhoods comprising San Francisco's Eastern neighborhoods, see There Goes the Neighborhood: a Demographic Survey of San Francisco's Eastern Neighborhoods, published collaboratively by POWER and Urban Solutions, 2004.

In the face of this agenda, working class African American, Latino, Asian and Pacific Islander communities are facing the prospect of complete displacement from a City that has been built on the land and labor of people of color. The cycle of displacement and growing inequity amidst tremendous wealth that we are experiencing is the continuation of a process that has been on-going for the last fifty years. It is not simply the result of one policy enacted by misinformed bureaucrats or greedy politicians. It is the result of local elite's need to compete within a global economy that is based on snatching the wealth created from the labor of Third World people, particularly women, throughout the Bay Area.

hope for the city by the bay

Although San Francisco's ruling elite has their agenda laid out and although they are closely aligned with other sections of the global imperialist class, they are by no means invincible. There is still hope for an economically, gender and racially just San Francisco. The success of the ruling elite's plan still depends on whether or not they can seize and control certain blocks of land and labor— two of capitalism's key ingredients.

The struggle over land in San Francisco shows no signs of cooling down. San Francisco's ruling elite need more space than they've got now in order to carry out their plans of regional and global expansion. Because of San Francisco's small size and high density, they will have to displace deeply entrenched, working class Chinese, Latino and African American communities. They need to expand the amount of commercial space available in the Financial District. To do that, the ruling elite will have to seize much of Chinatown. In order to expand retail space, they need to take control of the Mission and displace the Latino community. Both of these neighborhoods have been targets of gentrification in the past decade, and both communities have waged important struggles to stem the incursion of developers' capital. Today, both of these neighborhoods are in developers' cross-hairs, but it is Bayview Hunters Point which will be the primary site of struggle in the ruling elites' attempts to seize more land. This, the last remaining African American neighborhood in San Francisco, plays a central role in the ruling elites' plans to transform the City's political economy. From the construction of the Third Street light rail to the recent decision to give the old shipyard to private developers to the plans to raze the housing projects on the some of the City's most scenic property, the ruling elite are scheming to grab Bayview so that they can transform it into the bedroom community for the biotech engineers working in the Mission Bay industrial park.

San Francisco's labor struggles will likely take place in the trenches of the City's low-wage service sector. As the City rolls out the welcome mat to the expected flood of bio-tech engineers, low-wage service workers, most of whom are immigrants, will be shuffled through the back-door. Despite the ruling classes' efforts to shape the character of the local political economy and the face of San Francisco, they will require more low-wage workers to clean houses, raise children, shine shoes, guard important buildings, make food and prepare double lattés. The conditions that workers face in low-wage service work— hard work with little to no rights, respect or fair compensation— only look to worsen with local and state government's crack down on immigrant communities amidst rising racist, anti-immigrant hysteria.

If the sites of these impending struggles will center around land— i.e., San Francisco's Eastern Neighborhoods— and labor—i.e., low-wage service work— this means that the leading forces against the ruling class' agenda in San Francisco will be the African American, Latino, Asian and Pacific Islander communities. While all of these communities are similarly targeted, the way that these attacks are manifested is very different in each community. For example, one of the central challenges in the Latino and Asian Pacific Islander communities is over-work and low-wages. In California, the issues of under-employment and the informal workforce are intertwined with issues of immigration. Meanwhile, in the Black community, problems center around the lack of jobs and high rates of unemployment and the record-setting rates of the state's incarceration of African American men and women. While many African Americans in Bayview own their homes, most Latino immigrants are renters. The situations often look different but they are all connected to the ruling elite's deliberate under-development and super-exploitation of working class people of color, a core feature of the imperialist political economy. That different communities face different aspects of the imperialists attacks frequently gives rise to hostility between the communities of color and represents a serious challenge to conscious organizers attempting to unite these communities which share so much in common.

For better or for worse, none of these communities is strong enough to withstand the attacks that the ruling elites will surely unleash. These communities can only be saved if a strong alliance led by the City's working class African American, Latino, Asian and Pacific Islander communities can be forged because together they are strategically located in sites where the ruling elite is most vulnerable and together these communities have the numbers required to exert the necessary level of power. If properly organized and united, workers and tenants from key working class communities of color are positioned to resist the ruling elite's brand of U.S.-led imperialism. It will require this type of alliance to wield the power necessary to ensure that San Francisco is a place where low-income people can work, raise their families and live in dignity and self-determination. Undoubtedly, the ruling elite will try to dismantle any attempt to build such an alliance. They will pit communities against one another, playing off of the real differences that exist between them, and while uniting these communities promises to be a difficult task, it is absolutely necessary if the ruling elites' plans are to be stopped.

> If properly organized and united, workers and tenants from key working class communities of color are positioned to resist the ruling elite's brand of U.S.-led imperialism. It will require this type of alliance to wield the power necessary to ensure that San Francisco is a place where low-income people can work, raise their families and live in dignity and self-determination.

Although building this alliance will be difficult, understanding the nature of the political economy provides conscious organizers with the tools necessary to forge real and lasting alliances. Along with this understanding of the fundamental inequity of the existing system, we must also be able to articulate our communities' visions for a San Francisco that promotes the self-determination of all working class communities and communities of color.

chapterthree
anti-imperialist vision

nosotros nacimos de la noche,
en ella vivimos,
moriremos en ella.
pero la luz será mañana para los demás.
para todos aquellos que hoy lloran en la noche,
para quienes les niega el día.
para todos la luz,
para todos todo.

Nuestra lucha es por la vida,
y el mal gobierno oferta muerte como futuro.
Nuestra lucha es por la justicia,
y el mal gobierno se llena de criminales y asesinos.
Nuestra lucha es por un trabajo justo y digno,
y el mal gobierno compra y vende cuerpos y vergüenzas.

Nuestra lucha es por la paz,
y el mal gobierno anuncia guerra y destrucción.
Nuestra lucha es por el respeto a nuestro derecho a gobernar
y gobernarnos,
y el mal gobierno impone a los más la ley de los menos.
Techo, Tierra, Trabajo, Pan, Salud, Educación,
Independencia, Democracia, Libertad.
Estas fueron nuestras demandas en la larga noche de los 500 años.
Estas son, hoy, nuestras exigencias.

— Clandestine Revolutionary Indigenous Committee
General Command of the Zapatista Army of National Liberation (EZLN)[1]

Under the political economy of U.S.-led imperialism, San Francisco's dilemma never ends. The Madonna of world cities must always strive to remain "in vogue" to maintain her position within the global and regional imperialist economy. Local politicians and the private sector work hand-in-hand to shape San Francisco's future. Most of the time, the plans of the ruling elite don't benefit the majority of San Franciscans. In fact, they're not designed to. They are created simply for the purpose of preserving their privileged status. In carrying out their plans, the elites of San Francisco threaten the very fabric of the city and the people who live within its borders.

Although San Francisco's history and its cast of characters may be unique, the process of gentrification, displacement and extreme profiteering that we are experiencing is not something particular to San Francisco alone. This dynamic of destroying the fabric of communities in order to benefit a small number of people is common practice of the imperialist class everywhere, which raises the question: How do they get away with it? How does the ruling class manage to advance an agenda in which whole sections of society stand to lose as a result? Amilcar Cabral, the great revolutionary leader of Guinea-Bissau, answered this question by saying' "History teaches us that certain circumstances make it very easy for foreign people to impose their dominion. But history also teaches us that no matter what the material aspects of that domination, it can only be preserved by a permanent and organized control of the dominated people's cultural life; otherwise it cannot be definitively implanted without killing a significant part of the

---

' We heard excerpts of this manifesto, read by Subcomandate Insurgente Marcos, on Mano Chao's albums "Radio Bemba" and "Clandestino: Esperando La Ultima Ola...." The slogan, Para Todos Todo, inspired us in the development of our platform, using it as a closing slogan for one of the points within the Towards Land, Work and Power Platform. Translation of the quote is as follows: "We were born in the night, we live there, we will die there. But the light, shall tomorrow be for the rest, for all those who now weep in the darkness, for those who have been denied the light of day. For everyone, light. For everyone, everything. Our struggle is for life, and the bad government offers death as a future. Our struggle is for justice, and the bad government fills itself with criminals and murderers. Our struggle is for peace, and the bad government announces war and destruction. Our struggle is for the respect to our right to govern and govern ourselves, and the bad government imposes the law of the few on the many. Housing, Land, Work, Bread, Health, Education, Independence, Democracy, Liberty. These were our demands in the long night of the last 500 years. Today, these are our exigencies."

population."[2] Our study and our experience leads us to agree. An economically dominant class rules through the process of hegemony. Hegemony is the ongoing process in which a dominant class exercises cultural, political and ideological leadership over allied and subordinate groups, utilizing the combination of force, concessions and winning people over to manufacture consent.[3] The imperialist ruling class invests an enormous amount of time and resources to get the majority of the population to consent to and to carry out their agenda. This happens globally, nationally and locally in obvious and subtle ways. To better understand how they do it, let's take the example of the local elites of San Francisco.

manUFacTURing consent

Despite the City's reputation as a progressive mecca, the ruling elites of San Francisco do not shy from employing the means of force to rule— from bringing in the National Guard with orders to 'shoot to kill' during the 1966 uprisings in Hunter's Point, to using the San Francisco Police Department to systematically harass homeless people. When push comes to shove, San Francisco's ruling class is willing and able to show working people who's boss.[4]

While the ruling class is willing to unleash savage violence when they have no other option, state-sanctioned force isn't a sustainable way to rule if that regime wants to present itself as a democracy. When they have the option, the ruling elite prefer to

[2] Amilcar Cabral, "National Liberation and Culture." Address at University of Syracuse, February 20, 1970.

[3] Special thanks to the Gramsci Study Group and in particular Genevieve Negrón-Gonzales for her leadership in the process, which deepened our understanding of hegemony. David Forgacs, The Antonio Gramsci Reader. Selected Writings 1916 – 1935, p. 423 Raymond Williams, Marxism and Literature, Oxford University Press, New York. p. 108-114.

[4] The 1966 uprisings erupted in response to the death of a 16 year-old boy who was shot in the back by San Francisco police. An example of the institutionalized harassment of homeless people is the MATRIX program. Instituted by Mayor Frank Jordan from 1993 – 1996, the program involved escalated police harassment of homeless people issuing citations, confiscating and destroying people's belongings. Jordan reached the point to where he was pushing to even make sitting on the sidewalk illegal. For more information on the history of police harassment of homeless and poor people, visit the Coalition on Homelessness website, (www.sf-homeless-coalition.org/civilrights.html).

win over allies and quell class struggle by offering compromises. Generally, these compromises come in the form of concessions like wage increases, tax breaks, workplace protections, etc. They are not limited to being, but they tend to be economic in nature. Although they can dramatically improve the lives of working class people who are struggling to stay out of poverty, these concessions are never enough to make a serious dent in the imperialists' profit. In San Francisco, some examples of concessions are the cost of living increases for the welfare programs, the legalization of gay marriage or sanctuary city status for immigrants and refugees. The ruling class never gives up these concessions out of altruism; concessions are produced when oppressed groups raise the level of struggle. The ruling class doesn't just grant them out of kindheartedness. Like Abolitionist Frederick Douglass said, "Power concedes nothing without a demand."[5]

On the day to day, they simply try to convince us that what's in their best interests is in the best interests of all of us. The ruling elite seems to be following the Vladimir Lenin's observation that "A lie told often enough becomes the truth."[6] Everyday, the ruling class takes full advantage of their monopolistic control on the means of communication. Billboards, television, radio, newspapers— we are inundated with ideas that promote the interests of the ruling class as the interests of all. They propose their explanation of what's happening in society and how they think things can get better. Their policies are situated within a broader vision, to make their agenda seem like 'common sense.' Our constant task is to unmask the façade of mutual interest and expose as class biased the concepts of the ruling class that threaten our survival.

This is easier said than done. The complex configuration of hegemony is not exclusive or static. Hegemonic ideas, values and norms constantly change. They are re-created, and renewed; alternative culture and politics are permitted as long as ruling class hegemony is dominant. Class domination then, doesn't just take the overt form of a dictatorship; the ruling class also

---

[5] Frederick Douglass, Address on West India Emancipation, August 4, 1857.

[6] The Quotations Page Website, (http://www.brainyquote.com/quotes/quotes/v/vladimirle132031. html).

negotiates concessions in order to mask irreconcilable class antagonisms.[7] Underneath that compromise however, ruling elite hegemony conveys the message that resistance is futile and that their domination of the world is natural.

In our struggle to change the world, ideas are a part of the equation. Everyday, in our community there is a battle of ideas going on, and everyone takes sides. However, most of the time, we fail to articulate our ideas in the form of a coherent vision. This is an error on our part. It is critical that communities of color join the battle. Though the members of POWER's Amandla Project understood the root of the problems to be U.S.-led imperialism, we were unable to articulate our vision in proactive terms. Lacking this, we were consistently in a position where we took swings against our opposition, only able to hope that our work was indeed moving us forward. To make our hope more concrete, the members of POWER took on the challenge of developing a vision of racial, gender and economic justice. POWER decided to develop a platform that would communicate an alternative vision for the development of San Francisco and help us speak about the values of our organization to people in our communities.

Our process began in the community where we surveyed about 800 no and low-wage workers from across the city— single mothers, elderly people, day laborers, domestics, immigrants, General Assistance recipients, CalWORKS recipients. We did oral histories with San Francisco elders. Then we hit the books. We studied history, theory and statistics. Upon completing a draft of our platform, we took it back out and solicited feedback from people. The Platform was finally ratified by POWER members and community allies at POWER's Poor People's Congress which was held in April of 2004. The following is a copy of the Platform:[8]

---

[7] Michael Buroway, *For A Sociological Marxism,* p.224-225.

[8] We studied the South African anti-apartheid movement and were inspired by the "Freedom Charter." This document was adopted on June 26, 1955 by thousands of delegates from hundreds of organizations who came together throughout South Africa in the face of extreme repression from the white minority government, which used its control over the economy and the police to crack down on those struggling for the end of the racist system of apartheid. The "Freedom Charter" helped unite the movement and provided a vision for the movement over the next 40 years. You can find a copy of the original "Freedom Charter" on-line (http://www.anc.org.za/).

towards land, WORK & POWER

We, low-income tenants, unemployed and low-wage workers, declare for our neighborhoods, for San Francisco and for all the world to know:

- that a dangerous polarization is underway in San Francisco, just as it is across the globe. There is an increasing polarization of wealth, control and prosperity of a privileged few while the vast majority of us struggle with crushing poverty, despair and death;

- that we, the tenants, unemployed and low-wage workers of San Francisco, are overwhelmingly women and people of color – not because of any accident, but – because of the deep and historic integration of racism and sexism with economic exploitation;

- we adopt the following platform, Towards Land, Work and Power;

- that we pledge to struggle together, with pride and courage, until this platform has been made real.

THERE SHALL BE AN ECONOMY FOR THE PEOPLE

San Francisco is one of the wealthiest cities in the world, yet thousands of us struggle to make ends meet, unable to find meaningful work or laboring in jobs that work us hard but pay us little. This is especially true for women, as we do the work to raise our families as well as cook, clean, coddle and clothe the families of others and in return get only a few pennies and a lot of disrespect.

On the other end of the spectrum, corporations in the City rake in billions in profits, tax breaks and government contracts. Even though these corporations take advantage of public resources that belong to us, even though we do the work to make these corporations rich – we don't get our fair share or a say in how the wealth is distributed.

We demand the right to participate in shaping the economy. We demand meaningful work or income support for all. We oppose the continued polarization of wealth and power in the city that leads to our displacement. It is time that the economy of San Francisco put people before profits. All of the people of San Francisco shall have a share in the wealth of the city. *Livable jobs or livable income, now!*

THE PEOPLE SHALL HAVE HEALTHY NEIGHBORHOODS & WORKPLACES

For too long the elites of San Francisco have taken valuable resources out of our communities and replaced them with dangerous elements. Our communities are filled with poisoned air, land and water. Our streets are flooded with illegal and legal drugs. And when we go to work, we are forced to do the most dangerous and dirty work that makes the City function — without adequate health or safety protections. At retirement we are left with little to no support. That's why we see so many seniors living in homeless shelters or living in deplorable conditions in SRO hotels. To make matters worse, the elites have slashed funding to the resources that would allow us to make things better, like quality schools, day care centers, comprehensive welfare and health care coverage as well as other community services.

By stealing these resources, the elites have taken from us what we deserve. The people deserve healthy neighborhoods and healthy workplaces where we have all of the institutions, services and resources that meet the needs and hopes of all our people regardless of race, gender, national origin, language spoken or sexual orientation. We all deserve the right to determine our own futures. *¡Para Todos Todo!*

THERE SHALL BE LAND, HOUSING & COMMUNITY FOR ALL

Housing is a right. For too long, San Francisco has offered housing only to the highest bidder — those who fall short have been thrown onto the streets and out of the City. Now gentrification threatens to destroy San Francisco. The ravages of gentrification have destroyed countless communities of working class people of color. Affluent, mostly white communities remain untouched, enjoying the fruits of racist disproportionate allocation of resources. These resources and over-development are made possible because of the deliberate under-development of working class oppressed nationality communities.

The people have a right to live where we choose. Housing should always be made available to low-income people — especially people of color — regardless of our income. We have the right to maintain our culture, customs and community. After all, it was the labor of our people that built this city, and it is our labor that makes the city rich today. There must be a guarantee that any project for development will bring progress for the people. Our communities should be protected, not preyed upon. *We Shall not be Moved.*

THERE SHALL BE FREEDOM FROM RACIST POLICE & INS REPRESSION

A dangerous combination of reactionary patriotism and paranoia within the United States has permitted the escalating erosion of civil liberties and democratic rights of people, especially people of color, LGBTQ people and immigrants. These expanded powers give the state the right to spy on, arrest, detain and even torture "dissidents." With the creation of the Department of Homeland Security, the near merging of the FBI and CIA and the Patriot Act, 'big brother' is always watching. Whether we are born inside or outside of the U.S. Empire— Arab, Asian, Pacific Islander, Latino, African American and indigenous peoples— we are assumed to be and treated like criminals, terrorists and aliens. We are never truly citizens of this country. In our communities, the INS systematically terrorizes and deports people who have immigrated to this country. As a result, our communities look more like occupied territories than "the land of the free." All the while, the prison industry expands, willing and able to lock more of us up. *It's time that more resources go towards LIFTING our people up rather than LOCKING our people up.*

THERE SHALL BE MULTI-RACIAL AND INTERNATIONAL SOLIDARITY

San Francisco is not an island; we live in a global community. While we demand justice in San Francisco, we recognize that this can only come to be if there is justice throughout the world. Remember that many of the workers and low-income tenants who make up San Francisco were forced to flee their homelands in African, Asia and Latin America because the U.S. government destroyed their homes through war, exploitation and poisoning.

San Francisco must stand in solidarity with the people of the world and uphold the sovereignty of these nations, just as it must protect the culture and language of the people who now make our homes in this city. We demand the right to determine for ourselves the future of our communities. We come from different lands, speak different languages but our strength comes from our unity. *Solidarity Forever!*

THE CORPORATIONS SHALL PAY REPARATIONS

For decades, the corporations have taken more than they've given. The wonderful buildings of the Financial District are all monuments to the immeasurable sweat and toil of workers — from the Ohlone people to the Chinese rail workers to the African American dockworkers to Central American cooks. Even though they have been fattened by our labor, these corporations are not grateful. They demand more tax breaks. More wage cuts. More public subsidies. More and more and more. Those days are over. Corporations must pay reparations to our communities for years of slavery, exploitation and pillage. *No longer will anyone profit from our poverty.*

THE PEOPLE SHALL GOVERN & GOVERNMENT SHALL SERVE THE PEOPLE

Today, the government is controlled by a machine of elites who are not accountable to the vast majority of the City. The result has been the best government that money can buy. Under the rule of the elites, the tools of government are used to assist corporations in their non-stop quest to seize more and more profits and resources. The true point of government should be to serve the interests of the people. The government should work to actively guarantee that the needs of the people are being met, and where they are not, it is the responsibility of government to fill those needs. To ensure that this happens, popular participation in the policies and structures of government is crucial. The people should have the opportunity to make decisions that affect our lives, our families and our communities and to hold the government accountable for its actions. It is time for government to stop serving the elites and the corporations. *It is time for government to serve the people.*

'towards land, WORK & POWER' as counter-hegemony

As we have already discussed, the local ruling class is looking to advance San Francisco's agenda that fattens their pockets while remaining faithful to the designated role within the global capitalist system. In response to these plans and seeing the need to articulate some alternatives, we have intentionally developed our platform as a vision that is counter-hegemonic to this imperialist agenda.

In order to do that, one of our tasks in addition to mass organizing is to organize consensus for our alternative vision and advance that vision, "to make possible for tomorrow what seems impossible today."[9] We want to plant a seed in people's minds that resistance isn't futile and that change is possible through struggle. POWER organizes our own consensus and advances counter-hegemonic ideas in the way we wage campaigns and how we build our organization. In the following section, we outline the principal ways in which we see the 'Towards Land, Work & Power' Platform as counter-hegemonic to the vision of San Francisco ruling class elites:

UNDERMINES & DE-LEGITIMIZES NEOLIBERAL VISION
Globally and locally, the ruling elites have hitched their hopes to the political and economic strategy of neoliberalism. Professing neoliberal doctrine like religious zealots, they insist that privatization will solve our problems, that the market is

---

[9] Marta Harnecker, "The Situation of the Left," 1999.

self-regulating and efficient and that the unrestricted mobility of capital will lead to 'development.' When the imperialist class speaks of development, they don't mean the development of people, instead they mean the expansion of capital and increase of profit. Meanwhile, the state has taken on its new role with refreshed vigor, dismantling long-standing concessions and handing over public resources to the private sector.

In this country, it's assumed that if you have something, you've worked hard and deserve it. If you don't, it's assumed that you were lazy and aren't deserving. People are pitted against each other, groups are played off against each other— all fighting each other for the crumbs. The 'Towards Land, Work and Power' Platform is rooted in the understanding that there are enough of the things we need and deserve for everyone to live decently. It is the logic of the current system that prevents equal distribution of resources to all and ensures that the poor are forced to compete against each other. We want to create opportunities for all— not only for a privileged few. We seek to build authentic solidarity and unity amongst people through struggling together and linking where there are common interests.

Our approach to development prioritizes meeting people's needs, and this is articulated by the way we talk about the role of government in the platform. POWER asserts that housing is a right, and we demand accountability from corporations for past and present injustices, and that this takes precedence over a profit-driven, market-based approach. The organization advocates for authentic development, such as employment growth, decrease in poverty and the building of the capacity of communities and people so they may determine their future and achieve their potential. We reject the notion that what is 'public' is inefficient. Collective organization of society, as well as working together to meet our own needs, creates the conditions to develop community, culture and ourselves as individuals.

The ruling class strategy of neoliberalism has wreaked havoc on people all over the globe. The most basic rights— food, education, health care, welfare and housing— have been whittled away from those most in need in a time of growing unemployment and stagnant wages. In the name of 'adjustment' and 'development,' they have globalized starvation, poverty and death. In response, neoliberalism has become an international rallying point of resistance all around the world. As we continue our struggles, we must be guided by a vision of globalizing peace, equality and justice. As Cuban President Fidel Castro said, "Globalization is inevitable and historical. But we must fight for a globalization of fraternity and cooperation among peoples, of sustainable development, of just distribution and rational use of the plentiful and material and spiritual wealth that men and women are capable of creating with their hands and intelligence."[10] The struggle to defeat neoliberalism and globalize international solidarity is a core component of the counter-hegemonic, anti-imperialist vision we seek to advance.

RACE & GENDER – FRONT & CENTER

Many times people say that talking about race or gender in our organizing efforts is divisive, that it overly complicates things. They counsel that we should just 'concentrate on the issue' or explain that 'its about class.' Imagine a patient coming in to see a doctor. An incorrect diagnosis can spell disaster for the patient. Any competent doctor doesn't make an assessment based on just one symptom. She would examine all of the symptoms the patient is having, and then make her diagnosis. If a doctor has to look at the whole of a patient's condition, why then, would we as conscious organizers make half assessments of society's ailments?[11]

Beyond just making correct diagnosis, it's a doctor's responsibility to tell the patient what the problem is. We incorporate and highlight race, gender and all forms of oppression in our work, because doing so explains what's happening in the communities in which we organize. Concretely, this means that we intentionally highlight this within each point of the platform and in our campaign work. As stated earlier, class analysis alone does not explain the totality of the social ills produced by the system. White

---

[10] Fidel Castro, Speech at the CARIFORUM in Santo Domingo on 21st of August, 1998.

[11] POWER University 200 series, Session 2: Making Assessments.

supremacy and patriarchy have served as the foundation for the development of U.S.-led imperialism and continue to serve that function today. Could U.S. imperialism survive the due payment of reparations to African Americans for generations of slavery? Would the fair valuation and compensation of women's work, now deemed invisible, paralyze the system of global capital? The fact is that we are living in a white settler nation and the history of this racist, sexist, homophobic nation further escalates the need to lead our fights with a strong emphasis on race and gender oppression.

> Could U.S. imperialism survive the due payment of reparations to African Americans for generations of slavery? Would the fair valuation and compensation of women's work... paralyze the system of global capital? The fact is that we are living in a white settler nation and the history of this racist, sexist, homophobic nation further escalates the need to lead our fights with a strong emphasis on race and gender oppression.

Putting race and gender front-and-center in our vision provides space for us to explore and respond to the very different conditions that exist in different oppressed nationality communities. As the ruling class continues to mask and invisiblize the exploitation of women, lesbian, gay, bisexual, transgender, queer (LGBTQ) people and people of color we must see exploitation for what it is, and then must agitate and struggle against it. The 'Towards Land, Work & Power' Platform provides a framework which facilitates the development of campaigns and demands which directly confront the inherently oppressive nature of neoliberal imperialism.

CONNECTS THE STRUGGLES OF THE OPPRESSED & EXPLOITED

Imperialist hegemony promotes isolation and fragmentation. This serves the interests of the imperialist class by helping to keep potential anti-imperialist forces separated from one another. While recognizing the different histories and experiences of oppressed and exploited peoples, any counter-hegemonic initiative must look to connect struggles across their differences. While the conditions plaguing the Salvadoran immigrant community may look different than the conditions plaguing the African American community, our analysis of U.S.-led imperialism shows us that the underlying cause of those conditions are the same. All organizers inevitably face the danger of becoming too myopic in our organizing. There is always too much for too few people to do. This danger is especially prevalent in a social, political and cultural context like the United States where so much is done to pit communities of color against one another. However, if we hope to build a vibrant movement against imperialist destruction, then we must find a way out.

Because of the history of racism in the United States, communities of color need to build with one another, and that happens best through common struggle. The 'Towards Land, Work & Power' Platform gives a basis around which different oppressed nationality communities can come together and link their struggles. At POWER, the Platform has allowed us to build solidarity between immigrant Latinas working as domestic workers and low-income African American residents fighting against displacement. Because members of each organizing project see their struggles reflected in the broader vision of the Platform, they develop a connection to other people's struggles which are connected to the Platform's vision.

Still, the work of connecting the struggles of oppressed and exploited peoples must go beyond connecting communities inside the empire. Because forces in the Global South will play a leading role in the anti-imperialist movement, we need to connect our struggles to those of the people in the Third World. The Platform pushes us to do this. For example, the call for reparations is not one that's limited to the reparations owed to African descended peoples; it's a call that is equally relevant to the conditions in the Third World. The fact that Haiti is the poorest nation in the Western Hemisphere is frequently recited. What is not mentioned is that Haiti was made poor because France and the United States forced Haiti to pay so-called compensation to its former colonial master.[12] The call for reparations inside the United States must be connected to the call for the reparations that the First World owes

---

[12] Laura Flynn and Robert Roth for the Haiti Action Committee, "We Will Not Forget: The Achievements of Lavalas in Haiti." February, 2005.

to the Global South. The "Towards Land, Work & Power" Platform provides conscious organizers with the opportunity to connect struggles and break from the hegemonic norm of isolation.

PROMOTES SELF-DETERMINATION AND AUTONOMY

As conscious organizers, our work is to build mass organizations and working class leadership by engaging in concrete struggles that change material conditions while raising class consciousness. Because of the structural, global and historical nature of the problems that we face, the consciousness we are trying to build is not only about the survival of one individual, but is about the survival of our communities as a whole.

The under-development of nations and peoples is a central feature of imperialism. Today's constant conquest of land, labor and resources has resulted in the near re-colonization of nations and nationally oppressed peoples. This ensures less competition in the market and more profits to be made by those sitting atop the economy. The ruling class is moving to erase the idea that people should control their own lives and their own community; we see this as a danger that we need to respond to.

In San Francisco, the idea that African Americans, Native Americans, Asians, Arabs, Pacific Islanders and Latinos have a right to community has been further eroded as local and federal government increasingly turns a deaf ear to people's wants and needs. Culture is preserved only when deemed profitable for the right people. When communities demonstrate a level of self-sufficiency, they are targeted with the racist tag of 'blighted' and are subsequently 'developed.' The Fillmore is a prime example of this dynamic. But the state hasn't only leveled communities to stop self-sufficiency; any expression of self-determination has evoked a murderous reaction. This is evident in the murderous ways that the U.S. government dealt with organizations such as the American Indian Movement, the Black Panthers and the Young Lords during its counterintelligence program (COINTELPRO) of the 1960s and 1970s.[13]

In our platform we emphasize the need to cultivate the appetite

---

[13] Brian Glick, *The War at Home.*

and capacity of people to govern themselves. Whether talking about the role and actions of the economy or of the state, people should have the power to make the decisions that affect their lives. We look to examples like the participatory budget process developed by the Partido dos Trabalhadores (Workers' Party) of Brazil; an innovative example of how this can be done. Originating in the city of Porto Alegre, where in 1990 1,000 people participated, the process of participatory budgeting has continued to gain strength. In 1999 officials estimated 40,000 residents (mostly working class) participated in the process of creating a budget for the city.[14] It's now conducted in over one-hundred cities in Brazil. To fight solely to improve material conditions without addressing the fundamental relationship, role and process between people and the state is insufficient. We must promote the values of democratic struggle and self-determination and weave them into campaign demands.

Especially for those of us living and struggling in the cradle of MTV Cribs and Fox News, this will not come easy. The challenge of raising class consciousness is like that of a fish swimming upstream. It's not easy to forge the consciousness of the exploitation that is so central to the system when that same system is steadily pumping out ideas of consumerism and pull-yourself-up-by-your-bootstrapsisms. Nevertheless, the success of any anti-imperialist movement will help people to see themselves as a part of a class or community rather than solely an individual. How we conceive of what's possible in the world and our role in that process is shaped and re-shaped continually in the lived process of hegemony.

---

[14] Micah Maidenberg "What If Citizens Got To Decide the City Budget? Brazil's Workers Party Tries "Participatory Budgeting," LaborNotes Website, (http://www.labornotes.org/archives/2002/10/d.html).

A World Bank study found substantial quality-of-life improvements in Porto Alegre after the implementation of the Participatory Budgeting Process, including:

- Between 1989 and 1996, the percentage of the population with access to water services rose from 80% to 98%.
- Those served by the municipal sewage system increased from 46% to 85%.
- The number of children enrolled in public schools doubled.
- In poorer neighborhoods, 30 kilometers of roads were paved annually.
- Tax revenue increased by nearly 50 percent, a fact the World Bank attributes to "transparency affecting motivation to pay taxes."

Coming to recognize our interests and our role in making change happen are central steps in coming to understand that another world is possible. We believe the 'Towards Land, Work & Power Platform' is an important tool to help working class people of color to see themselves in new ways and to fight in their own interests.

chapterFOUR
where to FROM here?

Our strategy should be not only to confront empire, but to lay siege to it. To deprive it of oxygen. To shame it. To mock it. With our art, our music, our literature, our stubbornness, our joy, our brilliance, our sheer relentlessness ‑ and our ability to tell our own stories. Stories that are different from the ones we're being brainwashed to believe.

Remember this: We be many and they be few. They need us more than we need them.

Another world is not only possible, she is on her way. On a quiet day, I can hear her breathing.

— Arundhati Roy[1]

All too often organizers are pulled away from developing sharp assessments. There always seems to be another action to plan for, another house visit to do, another meeting to attend. With so much to do, organizers have little option but to drop something. If assessment is one of those things that is dropped, as it often is, then we find ourselves unprepared to develop a strategic plan of action that is grounded in the reality of the current conditions. Malcolm X once said that "the future belongs to those who prepare for it today."[2] We think that devoting time and resources to making sharp assessments today will allow us to position ourselves for the struggles that will come up in the future.

Having a counter-hegemonic vision of the future, such as the 'Towards Land, Work & Power Platform,' will be critical to the success of an anti-imperialist movement. It can help guide us, give us hope in the darkest moments and keep us on task. However, having a vision is not enough. It will take more than an inspiring vision of another world to bring that world into reality. Although *Towards Land, Work & Power* is not intended to be a strategy document, we will turn our attention towards the question of what is to be done now.

Towards Land, Work & Power is our attempt to develop such an assessment. Less than trying to develop a sweeping assessment for all of the movement, we wanted to demonstrate how a group of conscious organizers might answer three basic questions of an assessment which, once again, are: What's the nature of the system? What are the current conditions within that system? And who are the forces that have an interest and that will be capable of making change?

Although the imperialist system and the imperialist class sometimes seem invincible, the current conditions within the global political economy are opening the possibility for fundamental change. In response to the system's inability to secure the necessary levels of profit, the system is in crisis and the imperialists are in jeopardy

---

[1] Arundhati Roy, Speech at 2003 World Social Forum. Porto Alegre, Brazil.

[2] Wikimedia Website, (http://en.wikiquote.org/wiki/Future).

of losing control. It is this jeopardy that is the basis of the savage attacks that the United States has launched around the globe. As Venezuelan President Hugo Chávez Frías recently noted, "When imperialism feels weak, it resorts to brute force. The attacks on Venezuela are a sign of weakness," and as the United States attacks more and more nations, opportunities for anti-imperialist struggle are opening up.[3]

As we write this, forces throughout the Global South are seizing upon the opportunities that have been created by the current crisis of the imperialist system. Social movements in Mexico, Brazil, Kenya, India, Turkey and other parts of the world have all stepped up their respective struggles. The governments of nations such as Cuba and Venezuela have not only advanced their own models of alternatives to imperialism, they have also banded together to form an alliance which poses a direct challenge to neoliberal trade agreements like the Central American Free Trade Agreement (CAFTA) and the Free Trade Agreement of the Americas (FTAA).

The forces which are rising up today to challenge the imperialist domination are those of the Global South. As inspiring as these movements are, they cannot defeat U.S.-led imperialism on their own. The might of the U.S. military is too much to bear by one nation by itself. They still need a vibrant movement inside the borders of this country that demands the attention of the U.S. government. The problem is that where the movements of the Global South are strong and growing, the movement in the United States is weak and fragmented. If there is to be a concerted struggle to stop the exploitation and subjugation that is inherent to the imperialist system, the central task must be to grow an internationalist movement within the belly of the beast.

Although we did not write this book to provide a thirty year plan to the movement in this country, we do see three important imperatives that, based on our assessment, must be addressed to build a strong anti-imperialist movement within the borders United States: *1) build independent, fighting organizations amongst Third World people; 2) smash the state-corporate partnership; and 3) combat racist patriotism.*

---

[3] Hugo Chávez Friás, Speech at 2005 World Social Forum. Porto Alegre, Brazil.

BUILD INDEPENDENT, MOVEMENT ORGANIZATIONS ROOTED IN THIRD WORLD COMMUNITIES.

First things first. You can't have a movement without organizations. If our objective is to build organization towards a movement that focuses its fights upon U.S. empire, then we must root ourselves in constituencies who are strategic toward that objective.

Organization amongst who? The answer to this basic question depends on who within the United States we see as potentially willing and capable of making demands on U.S.-led imperialism. While the section of the anti-imperialist movement based in the United States will ultimately include a wide array of social sectors within the country, we think that there needs to be leadership from people with the greatest interest to drive such a movement forward.

Within the United States, as in the global situation, the brunt of exploitation falls upon people of color, in particular women. Informal, invisible and slave labor continues to provide the basis for the expansion of capital and profit, inside and outside the United States. We cannot ignore the role of racism and women's oppression within the framework of empire. With this assessment, we see the leading force within the united front against U.S.-led imperialism to be the intersection of the multi-national working class and oppressed nationality people.[4]

Cities play a critical role within the imperialist process of accumulation, functioning as centers of production, consumption and distribution and serving as home to high concentrations of working class and people of color. This is why we believe that within the belly of the beast urban centers will be the pillars of where we need to build up the resistance. If we are able to disrupt this process of accumulation, we will be able to heighten the imperialists' crisis and make the conditions more ripe for change.[5] This emphasis on building organization in urban centers is not

---

[4] Labor Community Strategy Center (LCSC), Program Demand Group, "Toward a Program of Resistance."

[5] This was demonstrated recently in Argentina, where thousands of unemployed and laid off workers forced their government to reject the structural adjustment plans of the IMF and the World Bank by laying siege to Buenos Aires and blocking transportation and commerce in and out of the city for weeks.

to suggest that important organizing will only happen in cities. Some of the fiercest counter-hegemonic struggles in the United States have emerged from the rural parts of the country— for example, the struggles of indigenous nations as well as those of the peoples in the Black Belt South and the Brown Belt Southwest, in the face of the nation's most racist forces. All of those forces have fought important struggles against environmental racism and the continued theft of land and resources by the United States government and some of the nation's most racist vigilante forces.

After Bush's victory in the 2004 elections, Democrats were left wondering— what do we do now? Some are now advocating to "go back to the heartland" to reconnect with Middle America. Others say progressive forces must incorporate faith into their politics. Based on how we see it, cities will be the central site of anti-imperialist struggle in the United States. There's a long-standing debate whether or not we can actually create a majoritarian movement in the United States. We don't feel hopeful. This is demonstrated in the election results of 2004. Those oppressed communities which decided to participate in the 2004 elections— and were not barred from doing so— came out resoundingly against George W. Bush. People of color understood and soundly rejected the Bush's agenda. Even if it were possible, even if we thought we could get white, middle class folks to sign on to an anti-imperialist, anti-racist, anti-sexist agenda, we don't believe that's the priority right now. The central task at this time is organizing those with the most material interest in advancing that agenda. As this movement grows, at some point all so-called Americans will have to decide if they stand with empire or if they stand for justice. In the end, the united front in the United States will need to have a broad array of forces. But first things first, rooting ourselves in strategic constituencies is the primary objective.

What type of organization? As conscious organizers, we must adapt the organizational forms and structures as conditions change so that they truly speak to and ultimately attract people. That's why the priority must be building independent, fighting, base-building organizations. By independent we mean that organizations operate independently of the Democratic Party and the American Federation of Labor — Congress of Industrial Organizations (AFL-CIO), the more traditional institutions seen as organizing or representing the working class. This is both to break from traditional structures in these institutions and the political leadership guiding these institutions. There's not much to say about the Democratic Party. As Talib Kweli says, "The mother—Democrats is actin' like Republicans."[6] They've demonstrated repeatedly that they don't fight in our interests. Their interests are with imperialism. Their perpetual position of retreat from public debate and our communities reaffirms that we cannot depend on them to represent us, much less solve our problems.

The state of the AFL-CIO is complicated and in flux. It has seen its membership plummet over the past twenty years, reeling from attacks from the state and economic changes. Recently, several of the largest member unions broke away from the AFL-CIO, bringing even more instability to that section of the U.S. workers movement. But even in the debate about the trade union movement within the United States, the issue of global justice was never at issue. It's as if the AFL-CIO didn't have a long and bloodied history of supporting U.S.-imposed dictatorships throughout the Global South, including the Pinochet regime in Chile and the Somoza regime in Nicaragua. Then, given the increasing evidence that the AFL-CIO was involved in the failed coup attempt against Venezuelan President Hugo Chávez in 2002, the silence of labor leaders in the United States is conspicuous.

New forms of independent organization in the United States have emerged in the last period, out of necessity given the rise of neoliberalism and the widespread attacks from the Right. Trade unions focus on worksite issues, engaging in conflict almost entirely with specific employers, rarely engaging with the state on issues outside of contract negotiation. However, such a focus on organizing members around contract negotiations leaves out a myriad of issues around which people were willing to fight. Worker centers, youth organizations, activist formations— there

---

[6] Talib Kweli, "Beautiful Struggle." *Beautiful Struggle* CD, Rawkus Records, 2003.

are multiple forms of organization that have stepped into this void and created new models that can respond to and repel the neoliberal agenda. Despite being smaller and less resourced, these new kids on the block have shown they can pack a punch. In New York City, the Taxi Worker's Alliance successfully organized a strike of taxi drivers, effectively stopping all taxi-cab service in all of New York City. Enlace, an international network of labor organizations, has successfully contributed to Mexican maquiladora workers gaining recognition for independent labor unions they've formed. The Tenant and Workers Support Committee in Alexandria, Virginia formed a $15,000,000 housing cooperative— the Arlandria-Chirilagua Housing Cooperative— benefiting 1,000 low-income residents of Arlandria through long-term affordable housing creation and community ownership and control. And recently in San Francisco a coalition, including the Chinese Progressive Association, the Day Laborers Program and POWER successfully raised the minimum wage from $6.75 to $8.50 for more than 50,000 workers in the City.

What is the organizations' outlook? As we build organizations, conscious organizers must avoid the trap of becoming narrow and provincial in our orientation. We are not building organizations to simply have more organizations. We are building organization to build a movement, therefore conscious organizers must bring a movement-building orientation to our work. We must look for ways to support the building of a strong anti-imperialist movement rooted in Third World communities inside the borders of this country that sees itself connected to the struggles of Third World people around the globe. This is especially true within the empire, where our true class interests are aligned with those of the Third World even when it cuts against our more immediate privileges. Sometimes this will mean that we should invest more resources supporting other organizations and the broader movement, while other times this will mean that we should concentrate our energies on building our respective organizations but never should this work undermine the building of the larger movement.

Cultivating a movement-building orientation is particularly important in the United States because the current conditions entice us to act in a sectarian manner and ignore opportunities to grow the movement. This movement-building orientation is especially important for conscious organizers in the United States who work within what is commonly referred to as the nonprofit industrial complex. Because nonprofit organizations in the United States depend on sanctioning from the Internal Revenue Service as well as financial support from the capitalist class, it is easy for committed organizers within this sector to become obsessed with promoting and sustaining their own organization— to the detriment of their relationships with would-be allies. There have recently been numerous debates on the limitations of organizations within the nonprofit industrial complex, but nonprofit tax status is a tactic which can be used badly or which can be used with subtle expertise. Given the nature of imperialism in the United States and the under-developed state of the anti-imperialist movement, it is a strategic imperative that the movement place a strategic priority on the building and supporting of independent, movement organizations rooted in Third World communities. The important thing is that organizations build themselves and their memberships so that they uncompromisingly see themselves as a part of global movement for liberation.

> **Given the nature of imperialism in the United States and the under-developed state of the anti-imperialist movement, it is a strategic imperative that the movement place a strategic priority on the building and supporting of independent, movement organizations rooted in Third World communities. The important thing is that organizations build themselves and their memberships so that they uncompromisingly see themselves as a part of global movement for liberation.**

A part of cultivating a movement-building orientation is making sure that organizations fight on the full range of working class struggles, against all forms of exploitation and oppression. While the power dynamics within the United States are rooted in the relationships of production, we understand that the oppression we face takes place throughout all of society's structures. At various times throughout history, the Left in the United States has focused so exclusively on the struggle of workers against bosses that it has marginalized working class struggles for national liberation, women's liberation and Lesbian, Gay, Bisexual, and Transgender (LGBT) rights.

For example, there is a tragic legacy of Left movements actually promoting homophobia and repressing LGBT activists. In the last ten years, there have been very promising developments in the Third World with the emergence of mass-based working class, LGBT organizations that are consciously aligned within national liberation struggles. The organizations Pro-Gay (Progressive Organization of Gays in the Philippines) and LesBond (Lesbians for National Democracy) are key examples of this new politics of class struggle, within the Philippines National Democratic Movement. These organizations wage struggles that address the material needs of working class, LGBT communities as part of the broader class struggle in Philippine society. Both Pro-Gay and LesBond challenge homophobia with Left, progressive and feminist forces all united as part of the broader movement for national democracy. In their website they explain, "ProGay-Philippines believes that gay liberation involves not just gay men but also all other people of different sexual orientations. Like other oppressed and exploited people, we struggle for social equality. We define the struggle for gay liberation as a part of the struggle of the Filipino people for national freedom, and at the same time, this has a distinct concern for the concrete demands of Filipino gay men. We advocate the full recognition of economic, social and political rights of all sexual minorities to freedom from all forms of sexual discrimination in family, the community, the government, church and mass media."[7]

Within the United States, we have to ask: what is driving the rise of anti-gay attacks by the reactionary right-wing in recent years? What makes LGBT communities such a threat to those in power? Each advance that LGBT communities have won over the last thirty years has been met with severe state-sanctioned violence and homophobic backlash initiatives. As we explained

---

[7] Pro-Gay Philippines Website, (http://members.tripod.com/progay_philippines/intro.html).

in the first chapter, capitalism is built on the foundation of patriarchy and depends on the invisible, unpaid labor of women. This stolen labor is so critical to the survival of the system that imperialism cannot tolerate any challenge to the construction of the heterosexual family. Lesbian, gay, bisexual, and transgender people are a massive threat to imperialism, because our very existence alone undermines the core assumptions that underlie patriarchy and the nature of the family. Hatred, violence, and the repression of queers functions to support the exploitation of women, by drawing the boundaries around society's definition of what it means to be a man and what it means to be a woman. The movement-building orientation that we are cultivating is one that understands that the struggle for national liberation, women's liberation, gay rights, disability rights, language rights, indigenous right, environmental protections and transgender liberation are all key parts of the working class struggle.[8]

SMASH THE STATE-CORPORATE PARTNERSHIP

Since the early 1970s, the way in which the imperialist class extracts profit has been transformed in ways that have a direct impact on the strategic targets and sites of struggle. In the last thirty years, the neoliberal state has become a basic tool to funnel wealth from the public sector into the control of the imperialists. This has allowed the ruling class to make up for the profits that they are unable to extract in light of imperialism's ongoing crisis. As a result, most working class communities and communities of color in the United States are literally being strangled to death, and those people within the United States who are best positioned to challenge imperialism do not have the resources to raise this challenge.

If the anti-imperialist movement's objective is to weaken the imperialist system while strengthening anti-imperialist forces, then anti-imperialists should focus a great deal of attention

---

[8] In addition to the organizations in the Third World, there are also key organizations developing within LGBT communities of color within the U.S., such as Fabulous Independent Educated Radicals for Community Empowerment (FIERCE) and the Audre Lorde Project in New York, and Transgender in Prison in San Francisco.

towards those areas where the ruling class is using the neoliberal state to stabilize a crisis-ridden system. This objective is particularly important for activists and organizers inside the belly of the beast, given the U.S. government's leading role in the global economy.

> **Anti-imperialist struggle does not only take place in the workplace— it takes place in prisons, in indigenous communities fighting against environmental racism. It's welfare mothers fighting for training and education, seniors fighting for adequate health care, families fighting for better schools.**

In previous periods of the development of imperialism, capital accumulation largely took place through transnational corporations. While these global monopolies still play a driving role in the world's economy, the degree to which nation-states act as extractors of capital is particularly acute at this point in history. The state's expansion of the prison industrial complex is an intentional mechanism to maintain and control the reserve army of labor. Corporate subsidies for the development of market-rate housing are little more than direct transfer of collective wealth into private pockets. Debt repayment by nations of the Global South is a globalized form of exploitation. And imperialist war is an important tool of controlling resources and expanding to new markets.

In response to this, new fronts of gender, race, and class struggle have opened up to limit the state's ability to act on behalf of global capital. The movement has responded to the neoliberal state by fighting the class struggle not only in the workplace. Anti-imperialist struggle does not only take place in the workplace— it takes place in prisons, in indigenous communities fighting against environmental racism. It's welfare mothers fighting for training and education, seniors fighting for adequate health care, families fighting for better schools. It's undocumented immigrants fighting for the right to drivers' licenses. It's low-income tenants fighting against the privatization of public housing. All of these battle-fronts are potentially important sites of anti-imperialist struggle where the people have the capacity to push the imperialist system towards crisis because all of these fights attempt to break the state's partnership with corporations at the same time that they look to improve conditions in low-income communities. In order to seize this opportunity, the people need to wage strategic campaigns which are informed by an understanding of the imperialist system.

We also recognize that organizing victories which raise the standard of living in the U.S. may result in greater levels of exploitation and oppression for those in the Global South. In our work locally then, we seek to develop this consciousness in making connections between the experiences of different groups and carrying the orientation to create global equity rather than to heighten imperial privilege.

COMBAT RACIST PATRIOTISM

In the months leading up to the U.S. War on Iraq, as the war-mongers of Washington circled the globe condemning that country, the world community weighed in on the issue. Millions marched demanding 'No War! U.S. hands off Iraq!' Polls showed overwhelming opposition to another launch of attacks. Several nations took brave and unprecedented actions, openly opposing the United States at the United Nations. How did the world's super-power respond? President George W. Bush scoffed, dismissing 10 million people as a 'focus group' and saying that America needs no 'permission slip' to 'defend the security of our country.'[9] Bush's dismissal of world opinion and subsequent waging of an illegal war on a sovereign nation that had not attacked the U.S. demonstrated the arrogance and chauvinism that pervades U.S. society. Imagine the concept: the United States, waging war as the self-appointed police of the world, above all laws and accountable to no one. Instead of reacting with disgust to the situation, the people of the United States increased their support for the president's illegal and immoral actions.

Through its machine of propaganda and hegemony, the United

---

[9] Richard W. Stevenson, *The New York Times,* "Antiwar Protests Fail to Sway Bush on Plans for Iraq," February 19, 2003; and *San Francisco Chronicle,* "Fired up Bush takes offensive President claims success on Iraq and tax cuts," January 21, 2004.

States promotes itself as the chosen one, destined to carry out its manifest destiny no matter what the cost to the rest of the world. The result is that many people in our Third World communities identify more with the imperialists of this nation, rather than with the people of the world. As Ho Chi Minh observed,

> In his theses on the colonial question, Lenin clearly stated that "the workers of colonizing countries are bound to give the most active assistance to the liberation movements in subject countries." To this end, the workers of the mother country must know what a colony really is, they must be acquainted with what is going on there, and with the suffering— a thousand times more acute than theirs— endured by their brothers, the proletarians in the colonies. In a word, they must take an interest in this question.
>
> Unfortunately, there are many militants who still think that a colony is nothing but a country with plenty of sand underfoot and of sun overhead; a few green coconut palms and coloured folk, that is all. And they take not the slightest interest in the matter.[10]

The success of the imperialists in promoting their own brand of racist patriotism produces two real challenges for conscious organizers working within First World nations. First, we must be careful not to contribute to the U.S. exceptionalism that tells us that the United States is somehow special and deserving of preferential treatment. Second, we must take care not to take a U.S.-centric orientation to fighting class, race, and gender struggles. It is easy for us to fall into advocating improving the lives of poor and working class people of color and women in the First World at the expense of the rest of the people of the world and of the planet's ecology. We must link our struggles for justice here with the struggles of people throughout the Third World. This is particularly important in the United States where the corporate media and hegemony machines have fostered a deadly combination of global ignorance and patriotic arrogance.

We can undermine racist patriotism by understanding our fights in a global justice framework. By framing our campaign

---

[10] Ho Chi Minh, "The Path Which Led Me to Leninism," *Selected Works of Ho Chi Minh*, Vol. 4. 1960.

and leadership development work within the context of an internationalist movement for justice, we can help Third World people inside the United States understand that our lives and struggles are inextricably connected with the struggles emerging out of the Global South.

The building of an anti-imperialist front within the United States is the central task of conscious organizers in the belly of the beast. To carry this work out, movement organizations must address these three areas. The form and character of what the work will look like within each of these areas will be different depending on the local conditions and the specific constituency with which an organization is building.

It is imperative that organizers and activists in the United States roll up our sleeves and get to work, building the movement that the world is waiting for. The conditions in the world situation are rapidly shifting to open the possibility for fundamental change to take place. If we drop the ball, the prospect for success is dim. But if we manage to build a movement led by conscious forces in Third World communities, we stand a chance to allow humanity to free itself from under the boot of imperialism. The choice is ours, and the whole world is counting on us.

conclusion

The world is in peril. The very survival of humanity is at stake and either we dismantle imperialism or imperialism destroys the planet— this is our dilemma.

Today, [we are] confronted with a crossroad which would urge us to make a collective decision, a decision to change the social order to save life on this planet, to achieve survival, social progress and equality, and what is for many utopia, or on the contrary, confronted with this dilemma, not being capable of make real changes, we would allow the end of life on this planet...

We don't have centuries in front of us, it could be decades at most that are left for the peoples of this planet to make a decision. We really change the social and economic order, we give real form, viability and outlet for a new, renovated socialism of the 21st century, or we decide that life finishes on this planet...

Because of this... I believe it is time that we take up with courage and clarity a political, social, collective and ideological offensive across the world... I don't think we have much time.

— Hugo Chávez Frías'

Although the sentiments that President Chávez speaks to in this chapter's opening quotation have been voiced by other thinkers— including Karl Marx and Rosa Luxemburg— they have never been more accurate than they are now. The current situation for imperialists and the growing discontent by all those affected has the oppressed and their oppressors on a collision course.

It is very likely that within the next fifty years, the future of humanity and of the planet will be decided. The imperialists are on the offensive, which means that for us there is no time to waste. Social movements in the Global South have gained strength from decades of struggle and rising discontent against neoliberal policy from Washington. The strength and potential of these movements have been demonstrated by their success at advancing demands and winning real changes, frequently targeting institutions such as the World Bank and the International Monetary Fund. From Venezuela to India, from Brazil to South Africa, from China to Bali, social movements and growing economies throughout the Third World are mounting a serious challenge to U.S. imperialist hegemony.

It is time that those of us living and struggling inside the belly of the beast engage in our work with a renewed sense of urgency. In the immortal words of De La Soul, "The stakes is high."[2] Our successes or failures will directly impact the outcome of this historic conflict. Although we do not have the movement that we need, we do see reason for hope. Periodically, POWER gets invited to attend gatherings and conferences which bring together community-based organizations from across the United States. From these experiences and many others, it has become clear to us that many organizers and organizations are grappling with the same questions and challenges that prompted us to write this book. Essentially, we are all trying to wrap our heads around a situation that is worsening before our eyes so that we can figure out how we can intervene and make change.

---

[1] Hugo Chávez Frías, Speech at 2005 World Youth Festival, Caracas, Venezuela.

[2] De La Soul, "Stakes is High." *Stakes is High* CD, Tommy Boy Records, 1996.

The process of writing this book and clarifying our vision has been positive and has strengthened our organization and has made us better organizers. It has built up our unity with one another and has deepened our understanding of the difficult tasks ahead. All four of us are convinced that we are on the right path. In the coming months and years, we are committed to continuing to tackle these questions so that we might improve the theory and practice of our work. We hope this book sparks discussion that will lead to further development of our theory and practice as conscious organizers and towards a long-term strategy. The movement's success will be tied to our ability to both touch upon the issues that move communities in order to build mass base and to understand the local and global terrain in which we struggle; making our adversary weaker as we grow stronger. We have our work cut out for us.

We must defy convention and continue to dream, as expressed by former-Sandinista militant Gioconda Belli, "I dare say, after the life I have lived, that there is nothing quixotic or romantic in wanting to change the world. It is possible. It is the age old vocation of all of humanity. I can't think of a better life than one dedicated to passion, to dreams, to the stubbornness that defies chaos and disillusionment. Our world, filled with possibilities, is and will be the result of the efforts offered by us, its inhabitants."[3]

In the constellation of movements, we look towards the direction of our comrades in the Global South, whose inspirational struggles light our path here in the belly of the beast. Here, inside the empire we have a task at hand. We must not fail. We owe it to ourselves, to the world and to future generations to chart our own path of resistance and do the necessary work so that we can become a beacon of hope, showing the empire and the entire world that within the belly of the beast, the fire of rebellion has been sparked.

---

[3] Gioconda Belli, *The Country Under My Skin.*